PET LIBRARY'S

Collie

Guide

PET LIBRARY'S

Collie

Guide

by Anne Young

England

THE PET LIBRARY LTD

The Pet Library Ltd.,
Subsidiary of Sternco In-
dustries Inc., 50 Cooper
Square, New York, N.Y.
Exclusive Canadian Dis-
tributor: Hartz Mountain
Pet Supplies Limited,
1125 Talbot Street, St.
Thomas, Ontario, Canada.
Exclusive United King-
dom Distributor: The Pet
Library (London) Ltd.,
30 Borough High Street,
London S.E. 1.

Printed in the Netherlands

Table of Contents

I Why a Collie   page 11

II The Collie's History   page 17

Collie Tales – The Collie in America

III Standards of the Breed   page 27

The American Standard – Head – Eyes – Ears – Neck – Body – Legs – Gait – Tail – Coat – Color – Size – Expression – Smooth Collie
The English Standard – Characteristics – General Appearance – Head and Skull – Eyes – Ears – Mouth – Neck – Forequarters – Body – Hindquarters – Feet – Tail – Coat – Color – Weight and Size – Faults
Smooth Collie – Head – Teeth – Eyes – Ears – Neck – Back – Forelegs – Hind legs – Feet – Coat – Symmetry – Height – Tail – The Two Standards Compared – Your Breed Club

IV Choosing a Collie   page 49

Male or Female – Spaying – Which Collie to Choose – Buying from a Pet Shop – Buying from a Kennel – Choosing a Potential Champion – Price – Age – Pedigree – Points in Selection – Registration Papers

V The New Puppy   page 67

Sleeping Quarters – Handling your Puppy – Sleep – Danger! – Feeding your Puppy – The First Night Home

VI Teaching Your Puppy to Behave   page 77

Housebreaking – Regular Routine – Urinary Behavior – Discipline – Chewing – Furniture Breaking – Jumping Up on People – Biting – Don't Steal – Outdoor Manners – Speak to go Out – Yard Breaking – Running Away – Dig-

ging Holes – Meet the Mailman – Awareness of Vehicles –
The Barking Dog – Puppy Walking – Come When Called

VII Kennelling   page 93

A Box Makes a Bed – Indoor Kennel

VIII Feeding the Adult Collie   page 99

Commercial Foods – Dry Dog Foods – Feeding the Stud
Dog – Feeding the Bitch in Whelp – Feeding the Nursing
Bitch

IX Training Your Collie   page 111

Equipment – Slip Collar – Heeling – Sit – Turns – Come –
Down – Stay – Social Behavior

X Grooming Your Collie   page 122

Go Easy on the Combing – Shedding – Ear Care – Eye
Care – Show Ring Grooming

XI Showing Your Collie   page 133

American Shows – British Shows – Ring Training

XII Breeding the Collie   page 143

Heredity – Genes – Coat Color Inheritance – Sable and
White – Blue merle – The Mating Season – The Whelping
Box – Personal Hygiene – Signs of Labor – The Whelping –
The Umbilical Cord and Sac – Intervals Between Puppies –
Eating the Afterbirth

XIII Caring for the Litter   page 161

Emergency Feeding – Tube Feeding – How Often to Feed –
Care of the Weak Puppy – Feeding the Nursing Bitch –
Feeding the Baby Puppies – Dewclaws – Difficult Births –

The Kiss of Life – Toenails – Weaning the Puppies – Ear
Carriage – Selling your Puppies – The Novice Stud

XIV Your Dog's Health page 185

Temperature – Inoculation – Distemper (Carre's Disease) –
Hardpad Disease – Tracheobronchitis – Leptospirosis (In-
fectious Jaundice) – Hepatitis (Inflammation of the Liver) –
Rabies – Rabies Treatment – Convulsions or Fits – Tonsil-
litis – Colds – Diarrhea – Bad Breath – Anal Glands –
Internal and External Parasites – Worms – How Dogs
Contract Worms – Whipworms – Roundworms – Hook-
worms – Tapeworms – Coccidia – Fleas, Ticks and Lice –
Eczema – Mange – Ringworm – Nursing the Ailing Dog –
Administering Liquids – Administering Pills

XV First Aid page 216

Restraint – Broken Bones – Sprains – Bruises – Eye Ac-
cidents – Stings – Wounds – Tourniquet – Pressure
Bandage – Shock – Artificial Respiration – Collapse –
Electric Shock – Drowning – Heat Stroke – Fish Hooks –
Porcupine Quills – Splinters – Skunk Spray – Poisoning –
Alkalis – Garbage Poisoning – Cyanide – Warfarin –
Phosphorus – Thallium – Paint – Strychnine – Copper –
Plant Sprays – Insect Sprays – Chlordane – Sodium
Fluoride – Ant Cups or Buttons – Radiator Antifreeze –
Chocolate – Laurel and Rhododendron Leaves – Sleeping
Pills – Choking – Burns and Scalds

In Conclusion page 231

Appendix—Dog Talk page 233

Cover picture: Tom Caravaglia

Earl Sherwan

Good Collie type.

I Why a Collie

Of the many breeds of dogs from which one may make a choice to-day, why, you may ask, should one choose a Collie. And it would be a fair question! After all, the American Kennel Club recognizes more than a hundred different breeds. Indeed, why a Collie?

The Collie is the family dog *par excellence*. "Right," you may say. "He is not for me. I have no family. I live alone". The Collie is the one man dog *par excellence*. He adapts himself to any kind of living conditions; his great desire is to please. He minds not whether he lives in a palace or a hovel. He minds not whether he lives in a household full of children or whether he lives alone with a single human companion. He does not mind whether he is the only dog in the household or whether he is one of many. He will fit into any kind of environment. There is one thing, however, that he does mind, and that is being neglected and idle. His ambition in life is to please, and he wants to do a job. But today, few Collies have the chance to do the job for which nature intended them, and so other

The Collie is the family dog par excellence.

outlets must be found for their great and undoubted brainpower and for their desire to be of help in any way they can.

Many Collies teach themselves to be useful. They do not need a great deal of training. The dog has an ability to think for itself and because of this it will often find its own particular niche within the family, and its own particular job to do. It may be just to accompany the children on their way to school, and to be there to meet them on their way home. Maybe there is an older member of the family, possibly one whose sight is failing; the Collie will almost certainly realize this and be on hand to help, for the person whose eyesight is failing may drop things and be unable to find them quickly. That need be no worry with a Collie about, for no sooner will something be dropped than he will know at once, and pick it up and hand it back. This is the kind of thing for which a Collie seems to have a peculiar sense; he will rarely need training to do a thing like this. For he will at most need showing once or twice, rarely more.

For many years there was an erroneous impression that the Collie was a vicious dog. This idea has died very hard – it is completely untrue. The Collie is an exceptionally trustworthy member of the canine species. I think this misconception comes from the days when every farmer had a Collie, and it was a rule that on a farm the dogs were kept chained up. Any dog chained for most of his life will develop a tendency to savagery. I don't blame him. I, too, would become savage.

The Collie is a dog with exceptional intelligence, as are many of the shepherd breeds, but I feel the Collie is different from most of the other shepherd dogs because he is exceptionally faithful, very, very sweet-natured, gentle, and has great depth of affection. He has a brain which seems to function almost in the manner in which our own does. Dogs, some will tell you, can't think, or can't reason. I am perfectly convinced that a Collie most certainly can do so. He also appears to have a very strong telepathic sense. This is something which is pronounced in many breeds of dog, but the Collie has it in the greatest degree.

For example, some years ago, there was a family who had a house in the country, while the father had an apartment in the city. The family also possessed a Collie. On Monday mornings father would leave for the city, returning late Friday afternoon. Meanwhile, mother and family, and the Collie remained in the country. Always on Fridays at about 4:15 the Collie would ask to be let out, and she would take herself to the station to meet her master at the train. Never did she need reminding that it was Friday and that it was

The Collie is exceptionally faithful, very, very sweet-natured, gentle, and has great depth of affection. These are some of the qualities which endear him to people around the world. This photograph was taken in Germany where the Collie is extremely popular.

The Collie has a strong sense of possession. This makes him not only an excellent friend, but also a protector. While not vicious towards strangers, he is not a dog who will readily make friends with them.

4:15. One day, however, she became agitated at 4:15 on Thursday. Her mistress told her not to be so foolish, but the dog took no notice, and so in order, as she thought, to prove the dog wrong, the mistress let the Collie out. The bitch went to the station and returned with master. Master had asked his secretary to "phone home" and say he was coming down a day early. This she had forgotten to do. How did the Collie know?

The Collie, while not vicious towards strangers, is not a dog who readily makes friends with them. He needs a while to think things over, using his sense of discrimination before deciding whether to accept a newcomer or not. He is a dog with a strong sense of posession.

As a watchdog, he may let somebody into the house, but that person frequently has great difficulty in being allowed to leave it, unless you tell your Collie that it is all right and the person may go. You can therefore imagine what could happen if someone entered the house illegally when no one but the dog was there. On more than one occasion a householder has returned home to a house which should have been unoccupied except for the dog, to find that his Collie has an intruder trapped firmly in a corner and is waiting his master's return.

I know of no breed of dog which so readily adapts itself to one's moods. If you are happy, he is happy. If you are sad, then he is too.

The Collie has a strong sense of humor. He does not mind being laughed with, but he does mind being laughed at, and he will constantly think up things to make you laugh.

"Oh, I couldn't be bothered with a long-haired dog in the house". How often does one hear this said? If only people would realize that it is very much easier to cope with the hairs of a long-haired breed, when the dog is shedding. The hairs of a short-haired dog are inclined to "sew" themselves in, either to the upholstery or to one's clothing. The hairs of a long-haired dog will lie on top and can be quickly removed with a damp cloth or rubber sponge or vacuum cleaner, and present much less of a problem.

There is also the question of a long-haired dog bringing mud into the house. This is perfectly true, and cannot really be denied, except by saying that the Collie instinctively is a very clean dog. He hates being dirty, and if, on coming home from a muddy walk, he is allowed to roll in a bed of straw, he will quickly clean himself. He will also help by using his teeth to pull off any lumps of mud which may have dried in his coat. If you are unable to let him have a pile of straw to roll in, give him a bed of old newspapers. These will serve nearly as well.

Another thing to be remembered when considering a Collie is the fact that this breed is almost entirely devoid of doggy odor. Their coats, even when wet, do not have the unpleasant "wet dog" smell that one associates with so many breeds. They are also not at all prone to ear troubles like canker, nor to skin diseases.

You may have the impression that a Collie is a big dog. This is not really true. Read the official Standard of the Breed carefully, and you will see what size he ought to be. If this does not entirely convince you, put an adult Collie in a bath; once he is really wet, he begins to look several inches smaller than he did when his coat stood out all round him.

Do I need to say more to convince you that the Collie is the dog of all dogs? Throughout the ages Collies have shown their intelligence and their devotion to their human masters in many different ways. In wartime they have been used as messenger dogs and as first aid dogs; in peacetime they have been trained as guide dogs for the blind. Their inherent herding instinct has shown itself at all times, for when they have been unable, as they mostly are today, to herd sheep, they find something else to look after – usually a small human being. You will find the Collie following its little master or mistress around all day, and that is why he appears so often as the hero of some fantastic story of saving the life of or at least of protecting a child from danger, be it fire, onrushing bulls, savage ponies, or the inevitable careless driver. Rarely does a month pass without news being received from some quarter of the world of a story in which a Collie is the hero.

Rudyard Kipling wrote, "And the woman said, his name is not wild dog any more, but the first friend, because he will be our friend for always and always and always". Could Kipling have been writing about a Collie? I feel almost certain that he was; for once you introduce a Collie to your family, you will have a friend for always and always and always.

To this point we have considered only the Collie's keen intelligence and sterling character. This is because had we stressed only the outer beauty, those who do not know the Collie could rightfully have asked, "Is all this beauty only skin deep?" For the Collie is beautiful – truly beautiful – from the dark elfin dancing eyes set in a chiseled head topped by gay tulip ears, through his lithe and yet muscular body alertly balanced on those graceful tiny feet of his to the plumed tail gaily waving his joie de vivre greeting. And all of this clothed in elegant furs – sparkling white apron and frosted point touching up a rich sable, or coal black or perhaps the aristocratic purple merle.

Truly a Collie stands out among other dogs as a Lion among lesser beasts, a King. You sense this as you walk down the street with your companion – in the admiring glances, the whispers, the admiration in the voices of passersby as they say, "That's a Collie. Isn't he beautiful?"

You will find the Collie follows his little master or mistress around all day, and that is why he appears so often as the hero of a fantastic story of saving lives, or at least protecting a child from danger.

The bearded Collie is a member of the sheepherding group, one of the three groups of dogs described in mythology and legend as long ago as 800 BC. As such, he shares a common ancestry with our Collie, although he is a separate and distinct breed today.

II The Collie's History

Dog. From whence did he come? How long has the dog-man partnership existed? These are questions which, unfortunately, are impossible to answer. If there ever were answers, they have been lost in the mists of antiquity, and in those mists they will remain. However, there is undoubted proof that there was already a man-dog partnership in the Neolithic Age, but I cannot help feeling that long before this man and dog had found each other.

In his earlier years, when man lived as a hunter, and unless able to hunt could not possibly find subsistence for himself and his family, then surely his partner dog was of tremendous help. I think that man must in some way have domesticated dog as early as that time. Later, with the coming of the New Stone Age and the changing over from hunting to pastoral life, dog must have become even more useful.

In the Chinese mythology and legend of 800 BC, dogs were already classified into three groups. One of these groups was that of watchdog. Watchdog surely not only covered the term as we know it today – guarding master and family – but the watchdog of early times must surely also have been guardian of the flock.

Surely one can imagine that early man would have given dog part of the food which he caught, and later, in return for guarding his flocks and his family, dog surely had his own corner in the cave in which he might live with a certain amount of security. Later, as dog became more and more domesticated and, one assumes, more gentle, losing a good deal of his natural, wild dog, savage ways, he crept closer and closer to the family, and was trusted to play with the children just as he is today.

It is strange that although the Collie must surely descend from these very ancient roots, no true description of one can be found until well into the middle of the 19th Century, and yet dogs of many different kinds have been described minutely in manuscripts two thousand years old. Assuredly Collies must have been used, or at least a similar sheepdog must have been used in those days, because we have proof of this in the Book of Job, where dogs are described as "sheepdogs tending the flocks".

It also seems probable that when the Romans conquered Britain, they brought with them dogs of some kind or another – almost certainly some type of herding dog – because an army rarely travelled without its canine companions. In those early days the only way to assure fresh meat was to keep it alive so armies were followed by herds of sheep and cattle. Surely dogs were needed to control and protect them.

Accepting then that these dogs came to England's shores from the Roman Empire, doubtless many of them remained there, or at least their descendants did, when the invading armies retreated. The immigrant dogs would then have been absorbed by interbreeding.

Later, when the Britons were again invaded, this time by the Scots from the north, undoubtedly the invaders would have taken home with them some of the Briton's dogs as well. They then would have been bred along with their own dogs in their farms and crofts at home, and gradually a sheepdog type would have emerged – the ancestor of the Scottish Collie. Generations later the new breed came back to England when the Scots herded their sheep over the borders to English markets.

This is the modern Border Collie, a type which is used world-wide for working sheep. There is no doubt that our Collie looked like this as recently as 100 years ago. Generations of careful breeding have lengthened his coat, increased his size, sharpened his nose and turned him into the beautiful specimen he is today.

The early history of the Collie is vague because, apparently, the dog was so common that few contemporary writers remarked upon it. One who did was Dr. John Caius writing in 1570. He has this to say about the shepherd's dog we now call the Collie:

> *Our shepherd's dog is not huge, and vast, and big, but of an indifferent stature and growth, because it has not to deal with the bloodthirsty wolf, since there be none in England.... This dog, either at the hearing of his master's voice, or at the wagging of his fist, or at his shrill and hoarse whistling and hissing, bringeth the wandering wethers and stray sheep into the self-same place where the master's will and work is to have them, whereby the shepherd reapeth the benefit, namely, that with little labour and no toil of moving his feet, he may rule and guide his flock according to his own desire, either to have them go forward or stand still, or to draw backward, or to turn this way, or take that way. For it is not in England as it is*

in France, as it is in Flanders, as it is in Syria, as it is in Tartary, where the sheep follow the shepherd, for here in our country the shepherd followeth the sheep, and sometimes the straying sheep, when no dog runs before them, nor goeth about and beside them, gather themselves into a flock, when they hear the shepherd whistle, for fear of the dog (as I imagine), remembering that (if unreasoning creatures may be reported to have memory) the dog commonly runneth out at his master's warrant, which is his whistle. This have we oftentimes marked when we have taken our journey from town to town; when we have heard a shepherd whistle, we have reined in our horse and stood still a space to see the proof and trial of this matter. Furthermore, with the dog doth the shepherd take the sheep to slaughter, and to be healed if they be sick, and no hurt or harm is done by the dogs to the simple creature.

Rawdon B. Lee, a 19th century dog historian, has traced the derivation of the Collie's name. He tells us that it was originally

It is not quite clear whether the smooth Collie was developed as a separate breed, or was a parallel development of the rough. The smooth was used more extensively with cattle, while the rough specialized in sheep. However, both have the same characteristics and the same desirable temperament.

AKE WINTZELL

spelled Colley, and that it comes from the Anglo-Saxon word for black – "col". The black-faced sheep of Scotland were once called "colleys" so, naturally, the dog that drove them came to be known as "colley dog". Shakespeare uses the word in its meaning of black in his play, "A Midsummer Night's Dream", when he says, "Brief as the lightning in the collied night"; and Chaucer mentions "Coll our dog". Our word "coal" comes from the same source.

This derivation seems simple enough, yet there are other old writers who question it. One would have it that the Collie is so called because of the white band around his neck, suggesting a natural collar. Another claims that it comes from the Gaelic since the word in that ancient language for a whelp or puppy is cuilean.

It was once believed in Scotland that the Deerhound, the Collie, and the Scottish Terrier are all descended from a common ancestor since there was a great similarity in the shape of the head, expression and ears of these three breeds at that time. Another historian has it that the Newfoundland played a part in the Collie's early development.

Rawdon Lee tells this story of a traveller in the Cumberland Lake district to prove his point that a shepherd was seldom if ever seen without a Collie at his heels. The tourist asked a native how many people attended a picturesque little church he was visiting. "Why," came the reply, "T'last Sunday that war ten cur dogs liggin' in 't porch an' the churchyard." From this, the questioner inferred that there were ten churchgoers since each would be attended by his sheep-dog or "cur" as the Collie was locally called.

In those days obviously, the only thing wanted was a dog of excellence as a working dog, whether as a hunter, a shepherd dog, or as a watchdog, and selection would have been made only on that basis. Certainly it was not until the mid-eighteen hundreds that any attention was paid to the looks of the dog. It was only in the latter half of the 19th Century that dog shows came into being, and from that moment on more accent obviously was placed on the physical beauty of the dog. It was in Birmingham in 1860 that the first show was held which catered to sheepdogs. J. H. Walsh, well-known authority on the dog who was later to write a number of books and magazine articles using the pseudonym of "Stonehenge", was one of the judges. There were only five entries, but one can assume that this was the first time that any of the progenitors of our present day Collie appeared in the show ring. Ten years later, at a later show in

Birmingham, there were still only 15 entries but among them was Cockie, a dog who was to become famous in Collie history as the founder of a proud line. Charlemagne, perhaps the most successful of all 19th Century Champions, was his grandson. Even today, there are Collies with Cockie's blood in their veins.

Collie Tales

To prove the breed's cleverness, Rawdon Lee tells of a performing troupe of Collies he once saw in London. After going through the usual routine of circus dog tricks, one of them pushed a ladder onto the stage. This was placed against the wall of a "burning" house. The Collie climbed the ladder, crawled through a window and returned with a "baby" in its mouth which he carried to a place of safety. The dog then fell over on its side, pretending to be exhausted.

Champion Coronation Merry Madcap, winning Best of Variety at the Collie Club Show of Southern New Jersey. He was bred and is owned by Isabel Chamberlin, Jeffersonville, Indiana.

Two other Collies appeared pulling and pushing an ambulance and carried the "dead" dog away on a stretcher.

There is another story about a Collie who could play "Nap", a common card game of the time; he was "so proficient as to be able to hold his own with anyone his owner challenged." Apparently, however, the dog knew which cards to play by a secret signal from his master.

We read that Collies were once used in South Africa by ostrich breeders to drive the birds from "kraal to camp" for plucking their feathers. The dogs handled their unusual charges proficiently, and although the great birds would frequently charge a man when angry they were cowed by the presence of the Collies.

A black Collie named "Help" collected for a charitable fund on the railroads of the period. On his collar was inscribed, "I am Help, the Railway Dog of England, and Travelling Agent for the Orphans of the Railway Men Killed on Duty". The contributions he collected, it is claimed, were "incredible".

Queen Victoria was the proud possessor of a white Collie, which was rare then, and still is, comparatively. Collie fanciers of the time were afraid it would start a fad for White Collies but apparently their fears were ungrounded.

The Collie in America

In common with Collies everywhere, the American Collie of today owes his origin to his British forebears, and a debt to the American fanciers who so assiduously made raids on the home country and purchased some of the very best of British stock.

The first American dog show was held in Philadelphia in 1877, but no Collies appear to have been exhibited. The first record of Collies at an American show was in the following year, at Westminster where as in Britain they competed in classes for Sheepdogs.

Interest in the breed grew during the next decade, each show having more exhibits than the previous one, until, in 1886, the Collie Club of America came into being. As you know, it is still with us, and is thus one of the oldest breed clubs of any breed anywhere in the world.

Throughout this decade Collie fanciers repeatedly imported stock from across the Atlantic, and competition became more and more keen, while the breeding of Collies grew both in numbers and in interest. Imports during this time included such dogs as Tweed II, Ayrshire Laddie, Marcus, Champion Dublin Scot and Champion Flurry II to mention only a few of those whose names are still to be found behind today's pedigrees.

1894 was a near golden year for the breed in America, for it was at this moment that Champion Christopher, Champion Sefton Hero and Charlton Phyllis left Britain for this country.

During the latter years of the last, and the early years of this century many of the kennel names – household words today where Collies are discussed – came into being: the Chestnut Hills of Mr. Mitchell Harrison, Wellesbourne, which had started in England and which now came over, dogs, kennel name, kennel manager and all; Mr. J. P. Morgan's Cargstons; the Coilas of Mr. Ormiston Roy; Brandane (Messers Black and Hunter); and Imna of Miss Bullocke, to mention only a few. All these owners imported many specimens, some of them going to the length of returning their bitches to Britain to be bred, returning again to the States before whelping – one of the reasons why pedigrees between the two countries are so inextricably mixed! Remember, of course, that this was in the days before Britain found it necessary to introduce anti-rabies quarantine restrictions.

The year 1905 saw the arrival on the scene of Mrs. Lunt's Alsteads, and a few years later the ranks were swelled by Dr. O. P. Bennett's Tazewells, Hertzvilles (Mr. H. L. Hertz) and, for a short time, the Knocklaydes of Mr. T. P. Hunter, who imported the English Champion Weardale Lord, renaming him Knocklayde King Hector, under which name he readily became a Champion in his country of adoption and also made a name for himself as a sire.

The coming of the Great War in 1914 certainly made available to the American market a number of top class Collies who might not otherwise have left their native land.

History was to repeat itself in 1939, though it cannot be said that the Collies imported at that time made any spectacular contribution to tbe American fancy, by then very well established in its own particularly successful bloodlines.

All Collies, everywhere in the world today, owe their inception to Champion Trefoil who, whelped in 1873, is behind every one of today's Collies in tail male.

Five generations from Trefoil comes Champion Christopher (1887) and through his two sons, Champion Stracathro Ralph and Edgbaston Marvel, we trace American Collie history today. From the

This is the outstanding merle stud, Bibarcy's Blueberry Alamode. He is owned by A. & M. Pedersen of Council Bluffs, Iowa.

former came Champion Anfield Model, a much lauded import who, excelling in many show points, particularly in head qualities, failed to pass on and was a near "flop" as a stud dog. However, Stracathro Ralph, through his son, Heather Ralph, was responsible eleven generations later for Champion Magnet, to whom can be traced the major portion of top winning Collies of today in the U.S.A., Europe, and Britain. Christopher's other son, Edgbaston Marvel, gave the breed four generations later Champion Parbold Piccolo, sire of Champion Anfield Model, but of much greater significance was his other son, Parbold Pierrot, who had a much greater influence on the breed.

To Piccolo today we trace the Bellhavens and their direct descendents, but to the Champion Magnet line we can trace almost all the top winners in the American show ring of this decade. Through Champion Laund Legislator we get the Lodestones, Hertzvilles, Hazeljanes, Noranda and some of the Brandwynes. But it is the other line, through Champion Poplar Perfection's son Champion Eden (later Alstead) Emerald that carries the main part of today's American Collie history: Brandwyne, Alstead, Sterling, Honeybrook, Starberry, Accalia, Silver-Ho, Parader, Tokalon, Erin's Own, Royal Rock and Glenhill, to mention only a few of today's top kennels.

It really seems quite amazing that Magnet should have had such a very great influence as a sire in America, for he was already nine years of age before he reached these shores and one would have expected that his greatest days as a sire were over, especially, since he had been widely used as a sire in Britain before he left and it is most interesting to note that the vast majority of winners in Britain today are also direct "Magnet" descendants, again through Champion Poplar Perfection.

No Collie history would be complete without the mention of Albert Payson Terhune, whose famed "Sunnybank" stories in the 1920s did so much to popularize the breed. Nor will any of us ever forget Lassie, the beloved star of screen and television. The original Lassie was, as is now common gossip, a female impersonator named Pal, engaged after many auditions to play the role of "Lassie" in the picture of that name based on Eric Knight's touching story of a Collie separated from her beloved master.

Pal, according to his owner and trainer, Rudd Weatherwax, was the runt of his litter, and was never of "Show" quality, although he came from good parentage. He was born in 1940, sired by Red Brucie of Glamis.

But long before Lassie, there was another Collie movie star – real name Blair, stage name Rover. Blair appeared in "Rescued by Rover" in 1905, the story of a Collie who saves a baby from kidnappers. So successful was this seven-minute drama that it led to three sequels, "Rover Drives a Car", "Baby's Playmate", and "Dumb Comrade".

The history of the Collie is by no means concluded and you who are reading these lines may well have your part to play. If so, one hopes that it will be played with as much dedication, patience and sacrifice as was evinced by those who have gone before and by their travail made our paths easier.

WILLIAM P GILBERT

This outstanding winner is shown winning at Westminster in 1967, the premier dog show in America. He is Champion Accalia's Mr. Timber, owned and bred by Mr. and Mrs. John H. Honig of Worcester, Massachusetts.

III   Standards of the Breed

The American Standard*

The Collie is a lithe, strong, responsible, active dog, carrying no useless timber, standing naturally straight and firm. The deep, moderately wide chest shows strength, the sloping shoulders and well bent hocks indicate speed and grace and the face shows high intelligence. The Collie presents an impressive, proud picture of true balance, each part being in harmonious proportion to every other part and to the whole. Except for the technical description that is essential to this Standard and without which no Standard for the guidance of breeders and judges is adequate, it could be stated simply that no part of the Collie ever seems to be out of proportion to any other part. Timidity, frailness, sullenness, viciousness, lack of animation, cumbersome appearancee and lack of overall balance impair the general character.

---

* *Published by permission of The American Kennel Club*   27

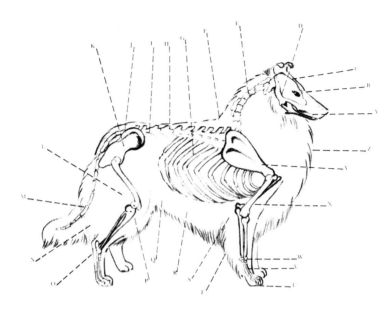

PRUDENCE WALKER

Parts of the Collie, and skeletal structure.

A. Muzzle
B. Stop
C. Skull
D. Cheek
E. Neck
F. Withers
G. Ribs
H. Back
I. Loin
J. Croup or rump
K. Hipbone
L. Thigh
M. Tail

N. Feathers or breeching
O. Hock
P. Stifle joint
Q. Flank
R. Body
S. Elbow
T. Foreleg feathering
U. Foot
V. Pastern
W. Knee
X. Upper arm
Y. Shoulder
Z. Chest frill

Head:

The head properties are of great importance. When considered in proportion to the size of the dog, the head is inclined to lightness and never appears massive. A heavy-headed dog lacks the necessary bright, alert, full-of-sense look that contributes so greatly to expression.

Both in front and profile view the head bears a general resemblance to a well blunted lean wedge, being smooth and clean in outline and nicely balanced in proportion. On the sides it tapers gradually and smoothly from the ears to the end of the black nose, without being flared out in backskull (cheeky) or pinched in muzzle (snipey). In profile view the top of the backskull and the top of the muzzle lie in two approximately parallel, straight planes of equal length, divided by a very slight but perceptible stop or break.

A midpoint between the inside corners of the eyes (which is the center of a correctly placed stop) is the center of balance in length of head.

The end of the smooth, well rounded muzzle is blunt but not square. The underjaw is strong, cleancut and the depth of skull from the brow to the under part of the jaw is not excessive. The teeth are of good size, meeting in a scissors bite. Over- or undershot jaws are undesirable, the latter being more severely penalized.

There is a very slight prominence of the eyebrows. The backskull is flat, without receding either laterally or backward and the occipital bone is not highly peaked. The proper width of backskull necessarily depends upon the combined length of skull and muzzle and the width of the backskull is less than its length. Thus the correct width varies with the individual and is supported by length of muzzle.

Because of the importance of the head characteristics, prominent head faults are very severely penalized.

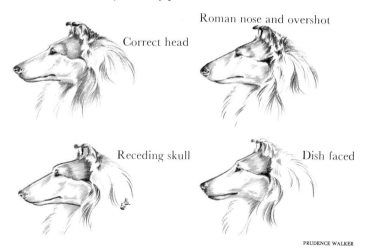

Correct head

Roman nose and overshot

Receding skull

Dish faced

PRUDENCE WALKER

The head of the Collie.

Correct eye and expression

Light round eye and weak underjaw

Small deep set eyes giving mean expression

PRUDENCE WALKER

The eyes of the Collie.

Eyes:

Because of the combination of the flat skull, the arched eyebrows, the slight stop and the rounded muzzle, the foreface must be chiseled to form a receptacle for the eyes and they are necessarily placed obliquely to give them the required forward outlook. Except for the blue merles, they are required to be matched in color. They are almond-shaped, of medium size and never properly appear to be large or prominent. The color is dark and the eye does not show a yellow ring or a sufficiently prominent haw to affect the dog's expression..

The eyes have a clear, bright appearance, expressing intelligent inquisitiveness, particularly when the ears are drawn up and dog is on the alert.

In blue merles, dark brown eyes are preferable but either or both eyes may be merle or china in color without specific penalty. A large, round, full eye seriously detracts from the desired "sweet" expression. Eye faults are heavily penalized.

Ears:

The ears are in proportion to the size of the head and, if they are carried properly and unquestionably "break" naturally, are seldom too small. Large ears usually cannot be lifted correctly off the head and even if lifted they will be out of proportion to the size of the head. When in repose the ears are folded lengthwise and thrown back into the frill. On the alert they are drawn well up on the backskull and are carried about three-quarters erect, with about one-fourth of the ear tipping or "breaking" forward. A dog with prick ears or low ears cannot show true expression and is penalized accordingly.

Neck:

The neck is firm, clean, muscular, sinewy and heavily frilled. It is fairly long, is carried upright with a slight arch at the nape and impart a proud upstanding appearance showing off the frill.

Body:

The Body is firm, hard and muscular, a trifle long in proportion to the height. The ribs are well-rounded behind the well-sloped shoulders and the chest is deep, extending to the elbows. The back is strong and level, supported by powerful hips and the croup is sloped to give a well rounded finish. The loin is powerful and slightly arched. Noticeable fat dogs or dogs in

The ears of the Collie.

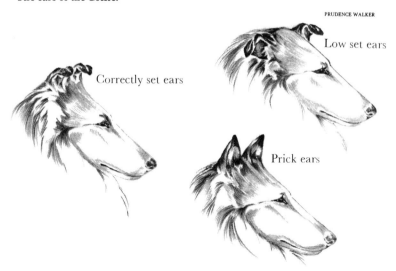

PRUDENCE WALKER

Low set ears

Correctly set ears

Prick ears

Before making a final choice, you should study Collies such as this one. He is International Champion Stoneykirk Reflection, owned by Mr. and Mrs. John H. Honig of Worcester, Massachusetts. Stoney is considered by many to be the top winning Collie of all times.

poor flesh or with skin disease or with no undercoat are out of condition and are moderately penalized accordingly.

In grown males a monorchid or cryptorchid is disqualified.

Legs:

The forelegs are straight and muscular, with a fair amount of bone considering the size of the dog. A cumbersome appearance is undesirable. Both narrow and wide placement are penalized. The forearm is moderately fleshy and the pasterns are flexible but without weakness. The hind legs are less fleshy, are muscular at the thighs, very sinewy and the hocks and stifles are well bent. A cow hocked dog or a dog with straight stifles is penalized. The comparatively small feet are approximately oval in shape. The soles are well padded and tough and the toes are well arched and close together. When the Collie is not in motion the legs and feet are judged by allowing the dog to come to a natural stop in a landing position so that both the forelegs and

Correct forehand and
shoulder placement

Skeletal drawing showing
correct shoulder placement

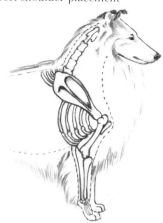

PRUDENCE WALKER

The forequarters of the Collie.

*the hind legs are placed well apart, with the feet extending
straight forward. Excessive "posing" is undesirable.*

Gait:

*The gait or movement is distinctly characteristic of the breed.
A sound Collie is not out at the elbows but it does, nevertheless,
move toward the observer with its front feet tracking comparatively close together at the ground. The front legs do not
"cross over" nor does the Collie move with a pacing or rolling*

Correct hindquarters

Skeletal drawing showing
correct hip-placement
and bend of stifle

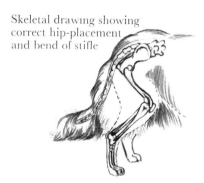

PRUDENCE WALKER

The hindquarters of the Collie.

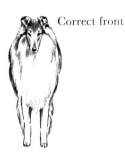 Correct front

 Out at elbow and pin-toed

Too wide and heavy in front

Too narrow in front and toes turned out

The Collie front.

PRUDENCE WALKER

 Cow hocks

Correct hocks

Hocks too wide

Narrow hindquarters

PRUDENCE WALKER

The Collie rear.

gait. Viewed from the front, one gains the impression that the dog is capable of changing its direction of travel almost instantaneously, as indeed it is. When viewed from the rear, the hind legs, from the hock joint to the ground, move in comparatively close-together, parallel, vertical planes. Viewed from the side, the gait is not choppy but smooth. The reasonably long "reaching" stride is even, easy, light and seemingly effortless.

Tail:

The tail is moderately long, the bone reaching to the hock joint, or below. It is carried low when the dog is quiet, the end having an upward twist or "swirl". When gaited or when the dog is excited it is carried gaily but not over the back.

Coat:

The well-fitted, proper-textured coat is the crowning glory of the Rough Variety of Collie. It is abundant except on the head and legs. The outer coat is straight and harsh to the touch. A soft, open outer coat or a curly outer coat, regardless of quantity, is penalized. The under coat, however, is soft, furry and so close together that it is difficult to see the skin when the hair is

Champion Coronation Powder Smoke, owned by Isabel Chamberlin of Jeffersonville, Indiana, is a dog of which to be proud. Winner of Best of Show in the Collie Club of Maryland and Best of Variety in the Collie Club of Western New York Specialty.

parted. The coat is very abundant on the mane and frill. The forelegs are smooth and well feathered to the back of the pasterns. The hind legs are smooth below the hock joints. Any feathering below the hocks is removed for the show ring. The hair on the tail is very profuse and on the hips it is long and bushy. The texture, quantity and the extent to which the coat "fits the dog" are important points.

Color:

The four recognized colors are "Sable and White", "Tri-color", "Blue Merle" and "White". There is no preference among them. The "Sable and White" is predominantly sable (a fawn sable color of varying shades from light gold to dark mahogany) with white markings usually on the chest, neck, legs, feet and the tip of the tail. A blaze may appear on the foreface or backskull or both. The "Tri-Color" is predominantly black, carrying white markings as in a sable and white and has tan shadings on and about the head and legs. The "Blue Merle" is a mottled or "marbled" color, predominantly blue-gray and black with white markings as in the "Sable and White" and usually has tan shadings as in the "Tri-color". The "White" is predominantly white, preferably with sable or tri-color markings. Blue merle coloring is undesirable in whites.

Size:

Dogs are from 24 to 26 inches at the shoulders and weigh from 60 to 75 pounds. Bitches are from 22 to 24 inches at the shoulder, weighing from 50 to 65 pounds. An undersize or an oversize Collie is penalized according to the extent to which the dog appears to be undersize or oversize.

Expression:

Expression is one of the most important points in considering the relative value of Collies. "Expression" like the term "Character" is difficult to define in words. It is not a fixed point as in color, weight or height and it is something the uninitiated can properly understand only by optical illustration. In general, however, it may be said to be the combined product of the shape, and balance of the skull and muzzle, the placement, *size, shape and color of the eyes and the position, size and carriage of the ears. An expression that shows sullenness or which is suggestive of any other breed is entirely foreign. The Collie cannot be judged properly until its expression has been carefully evaluated.*

Smooth Collie:

The Smooth Variety of Collie is judged by the same Standard as the Rough variety, except that the references to the quantity and the distribution of the coat are not applicable to the Smooth Variety, which has a hard, dense, smooth coat.

Expression is one of the most important points in considering the relative value of Collies. It may be said to be the combined product of the shape and balance of the skull and muzzle, the placing, size, shape and color of the eyes, and the position, size and carriage of the ears. This typical merle Collie was photographed in Sweden.

AKE WINTZELL

The English Standard*

Characteristics:

To enable the Collie to fulfill a natural bent for Sheepdog work its physical structure should be on lines of strength and activity, free from cloddiness and without any trace of coarseness. Expression one of the most important points in considering relative values, is obtained by the perfect balance and combination of skull and foreface, size, shape, color and placement of eye, correct position and carriage of ears all harmoniously blended to produce that dreamy, yet alert outlook which makes the perfect Collie the most beautiful of the canine race,

General Appearance:

The Collie should instantly appeal as a dog of great beauty, gifted with intelligence, alertness and activity. With no part out of proportion to the whole he should stand with impassive dignity and his movements, governed by perfect anatomical formation, should be smooth and graceful. An abundance of coat, mane and frill with shapeliness of head and sweetness of expression, all combine to present a pleasing and elegant picture that will inspire and secure admiration.

Head and Skull:

The skull should be flat and moderately wide between the ears with a gradual tapering towards the eyes, the width depending upon the combined length of skull and muzzle, the whole to be considered in connection with the size of the dog. The muzzle continues in an almost broken line towards the nose and must not show weakness or be snipy or lippy. Below the eyebrow there should be a slight and perceptible, but not prominent stop which brings the bridge of the nose line slightly below the surface line of the skull. Whatever the color of the dog, the nose must be black.

Eyes:

Are a very important feature, and give expression to the dog. They should be of medium size, set somewhat obliquely, of almond shape and of dark brown color except in the case of merles, when the eyes are frequently (one or both) blue-and-

white or china; expression full of intelligence, with a quick alert look when listening.

Ears:

Should be small and moderately wide at the base, and placed not too close together on top of the skull nor too much to the side of head. When in repose they should be usually carried thrown back, but when on the alert brought forward and carried semi-erect, with tips slightly drooping in attitude of listening.

Mouth:

The teeth should be of good size, with the lower incisors fitting closely behind the upper incisors, a very slight space not to be regarded as a serious fault.

Neck:

Muscular, powerful, of fair length, and somewhat arched.

Forequarters:

The shoulders should be sloped. The forelegs should be straight and muscular, neither in nor out at elbows, with a fair amount of bone; the forearms somewhat fleshy, with pasterns showing flexibility without weakness.

Body:

Should be rather long, with well sprung ribs, chest deep, fairly broad behind the shoulders.

Hindquarters:

Loins slightly arched and powerful. The hind legs should be muscular at the thighs, clean and sinewy below the hocks with well-bent stifles.

Feet:

Should be oval in shape, soles well padded, and the toes arched and close together. The hind feet less arched, the hocks well let down and powerful.

Tail:

The tail should be moderately long carried low when the dog is

The White Collie is not necessarily all white, but it must be predominantly white, preferably with sable or tricolor markings which should be confined to the area of the head.

quiet, with a slight upward "swirl" at the end, and may be gaily carried when the dog is excited, and not over the back.

Coat:

Should be very dense, the outer coat harsh to the touch, the inner or under coat soft, furry, and very close, so close as to almost hide the skin. The mane and frill should be very abundant, the mask or face smooth, as also the ears at the tips, but they should carry more hair towards the base; the forelegs well feathered, the hind legs above the hocks profusely so; but below the hocks fairly smooth, although all heavily coated Collies are liable to grow a slight feathering. Hair on the brush very profuse.

Color:

Color and markings are immaterial, but other points being equal, a nice showily marked dog is preferred.

Weight and Size:

Dogs, 22 to 24 inches at the shoulders; Bitches 20 to 22 inches. Dogs 45 lbs. to 65 lbs., Bitches 40 lbs. to 55 lbs.

Faults:

Length of head apparently out of proportion to the body and head of the Borzoi type are to be strongly condemned. Weak, snipy muzzle; overshot mouth; heavy or gooseberry-colored eyes, and glassy staring eyes, are very objectionable. Domed skull, high peaked occiput. Prominent cheek, dish-faced or Roman-nosed. Body flat-sided, short or cobby. Weak long pasterns, out at elbows, crooked forearms.

Cow-hocks, straight hocks. Large, open, flat, or hare feet; feet turned outwards or inwards. Tail short or carried over the back, or twisted to one side. A soft, silky, or wavy coat, or insufficient undercoat.

Smooth Collie

The description and standards, by courtesy of the Smooth Collie Club, England, follow:

Head:

Should be in proportion to dog's size; skull moderately wide between the ears, and flat, tapering to the end of the muzzle, which ought to be of a fair length but not too snipey with only a slight stop.

Teeth:

Strong and white; the top jaw fitting nicely over the lower, and where much over or at all undershot, it should count against the dog.

Eyes:

Of almond shape, set obliquely in the head, and the shade consistent with the color of the dog. A full or staring eye is objectionable.

Ears:
Small, and when the dog's attention is attracted, carried semi-erect, but when in repose it is natural for them to be laid back.

Neck:
Long and well arched, and shoulders muscular and sloping.

Back:
Rather long, strong, and straight, the loin slightly arched, and the chest fairly deep, but not too wide.

Forelegs:
Straight and muscular, with a fair amount of bone.

Hind legs:
The hind legs should be rather wide apart, with stifle well bent, forming sickle hocks.

Feet:
Compact, knuckles well sprung, claws strong and close together, pads cannot be too hard.

Coat:
Short, dense flat coat, with good texture, with an abundance of undercoat.

Symmetry:
The dog should be of fair length on the leg, and his movements active and graceful.

Height:
Dogs, 22 to 24 inches; bitches 20 to 22 inches.

Tail:
Of medium length, and when the dog is standing quietly, should be slightly raised, but more so when excited.

This is a candid shot taken at a championship Collie match in California. The dog is being readied to enter the ring.

The Two Standards Compared

As you have seen, these two Standards vary somewhat one from the other. The Standard of the English Kennel Club is generally adopted throughout the world, except in the United States. Whether a country, other than the country of origin of a certain breed, should ever alter the Standard of the breed, is a question which has been under discussion for a great many years. In this book we won't go deeply into it, but we would like to call attention to the differences between these two Standards. Undoubtedly, the new Standard of the American Kennel Club is far more full, gives a much truer picture of a Collie than the English Standard. One wonders whether it is possible that, had the English Standard been more descriptive in the first instance, America would have found it necessary to produce its own.

However, as you will see, there is always the question of height, and that is something which had nothing to do with how the English Standard was originally worded. The very first Collie Standard

This is Champion Leeshaven Sonata. This outstanding blue merle male is owned by Mr. and Mrs. John C. Parry who consider breeding Collies a labor of love.

was drawn up as long ago as 1881; it was revised in 1898 and again in 1910, small alternations being made each time by the English Collie fanciers. In those early years the Clubs themselves were responsible for formulating the Standard for their own breeds, but in 1949 the English Kennel Club took over the job of correlating the Standards, and every Club was asked to produce one Standard for its breed, to send this to the Kennel Club when it was completed and from there on the Kennel Club took charge, taking the entire responsibility for the Standards. It took some time to achieve this, because, unlike most countries of the world, England is allowed a multiplicity of clubs for any one breed, and these clubs all had to agree upon the various clauses of the Standard before it could be passed to the Kennel Club. However, since 1949 it has been impossible to change any part of any Standard unless all the breed clubs for that particular breed are in complete unanimity and as

Britain has no less than fifteen breed clubs for the Rough Collie, one must assume that unanimity would be very hard to obtain.

As you will see, the main points in which the two Standards differ are those of size and color. The American Standard demands that the Collie of both sexes be two inches larger than its English counterpart. The English Standard is particularly vague regarding color, but one understands that in the English show ring the white Collie is taboo. In America, not only is the White Collie allowed, it is described within the Standard, and therefore no exception can possibly be taken to it. Reading any Standard can only give you a vague picture of a dog, but the American Standard is one of the most detailed there is of any breed, and careful reading, re-reading, and yet again re-reading, should give anyone who is anxious to own a really good Collie a shrewd idea of what to look for, but the best advice I can give you is, taking your Standard with you, attend as many shows as you reasonably can until such time as the Standard becomes for you a living dog. Then, and then only, is the time to think about choosing a puppy, at least if you hope to end up with a show specimen. But trying to judge a puppy by the Standard – because remember the Standard is drawn for an adult dog – is a very difficult thing indeed, and something at which one becomes expert only with many years of practice.

The ideal Collie head. English Champion Such-A-Struggle from Shiel.

SALLY ANNE THOMPSON

The noted dog artist, Prudence Walker, has drawn the ideal Collie in three different coat colors; sable, blue merle, and tricolor.

Your Breed Club

The first advice that should be given to anybody purchasing a pedigreed puppy of any breed is to join the parent club of that breed.

In various countries of the world there are different regulations regarding breed clubs. In all the Continental countries only one national club is permitted for each breed. In Britain there is a multiplicity of clubs for the different breeds, and at the time of writing there are no less than fifteen individual clubs for Rough Collies.

In America, there is the parent club, the Collie Club of America, and in my experience through many countries of the world, I know of no breed club which does more for its members and its breed than this one. It is not only the club for Collies in the United States, but it is a magnificent example of what a breed club should be and do. At the present time it has over 2,500 members, and I cannot believe that there is any club in the world that has a larger membership, or whose members get better value for their money.

In America, where there is a choice between joining the national club or the local club for your breed, my advice is to join both. The parent club disseminates literature that is of tremendous value to novice and experienced breeder alike. The local clubs do a great deal by holding meetings and small shows and they too disseminate information.

The few dollars which it costs to join these clubs is money well worth spending, but do remember that club membership cannot be all take, take, take. You must remember that a good club depends on its members for their help. Their are various ways in which you can help and your club will tell you what these ways are; so don't be just a taker and never a giver. If you are only a taker, you will not in any way get full value from any club you join because by giving to other members you yourself will gain a great deal.

While one may deplore the multiplicity of clubs in Britain, where it is a question of one against the other and there is no true parent club, one can also deplore the fact that in the Continental countries there is only one club for each breed. In at least two Continental

The Collie is a long-lived breed. This is English Champion Mywicks Meadow Lancer. At the time this picture was taken he was 9 years old.

countries recently, something went wrong with these clubs, and they are now under a ban from their national Kennel Clubs. In such cases the breed can only suffer. (In one country, the club for Rough Collies has been under a ban for no less than twelve years.)

One club per country does not appear to be a good thing, but neither, I think, are fifteen. Surely the happy medium lies somewhere between.

Anyway, it is up to you to join a club, to take from your club and to give to your club. In this way only will you reap to the full the pleasure which comes from owning a pedigreed Collie.

English Champion Dunmblae Dog Watch is an outstanding stud dog. Six years of age, he has compiled an outstanding record, not only in the show ring itself, but also for producing show-quality puppies.

The color of this sable puppy may change – and change quite considerably – as he matures. As a rule, sable becomes darker in color each time the coat changes.

IV Choosing a Collie

When the time has come for you to choose your puppy, bear in mind that it is highly unlikely two mediocre Collies will give birth to a champion. However, two champions do not always reproduce their like either. Quite frequently certain dogs have been tremendously great producers; dogs who were, in fact, not show specimens themselves but who had in their makeup some trait that they were able to pass on to their progeny with great probability. A dog with this characteristic is known as prepotent.

One cannot advise the purchase of puppies from completely unknown parentage. At the same time don't discard a puppy whose father was not a big show winner if you know that the father has sired many winners, or if there were many champions in his background. This particular puppy may, in fact, be better for your needs than the whelp of a champion.

Do try whenever possible to see both parents. Look at the good and the bad points in both, and make sure that they don't fail in the same points. Before choosing your puppy, you will almost certainly have decided what color you want, but don't limit yourself too much. By this I mean, if you want a sable or a tricolor, well and good – that you will know – but don't pass up a puppy just because it hasn't got a full white collar, or because the white markings on its front legs do not match.

Nowhere does the Standard tell us exactly how the dog should be marked; simply that the white marking can appear usually on the chest, neck, legs, feet, and the tip of the tail. A dog may also have a blaze on its foreface, which may or may not extend through to the skull. Quite often a puppy will be born with a blaze which will gradually disappear. Some people dislike a blaze intensely, but it should never be discriminated against unless, as sometimes happens, it is

All these puppies are so cute, it's hard to make a choice. As we can see by this picture, cats and puppies are not instinctive enemies. It's hard to tell who's enjoying himself more – puppies, cat, or children.

SALLY ANNE THOMPSON

wide or misshapen enough to detract from the Collie expression. As far as body color color is concerned, the tricolor, born black, will never change, but he may become slightly rusty as his coat ages. The Sable, however, will change – and change quite considerably – for nearly always, except in the case of the clear golden Sables, it will become darker in color each time he changes his coat, and the puppy that was a sort of gray or greeny sable as a young dog may finish up a gorgeous shade of rich mahogany. However, as the Standard tells us the Sable may be any shade from gold to deep mahogany, this is immaterial.

In blue Merles, however, the color is extremely important, for the adult dog must be blue. Therefore, never choose a puppy which has a tendency to a slate grey appearance, or with a muddy tinge, for he will not go blue. Very often, the pup who will finish the best color of all is the one who at the age of eight weeks appears to be black and white ticked.

The White Collie must be white in body, but do not choose a cream puppy because the chances are that he will never become truly white. The ideal White Collie is an all white dog with either a sable or a tricolor head.

Male or Female

Now that you have definitely decided the Collie is for you, the moment has come when you must make your choice. First, decide whether you want a dog puppy or a bitch puppy. Each sex has its advocates and its detractors. The main objection to the female is that she has periods of coming in heat, but with a Collie this is not usually quite so serious as in other breeds. It is as unusual for a Collie to come into heat at the regular intervals of six months, as it is usual with most breeds. I would say that the average period between heats in a Collie is ten months, but in purchasing a female one should always have regard to the fact that for the bitch's own health it is wise, in my opinion, to let her have a litter at least once in her lifetime.

Spaying

However, in some countries and particularly in America, it is now a usual thing for a bitch puppy to be spayed, either while still the

Whether to buy a male or female is a matter for the individual to decide. The important thing is that you love your puppy and your puppy loves you.

property of her breeder, or after her purchase. This is best done by her new owner when she is about six months old. The operation of spaying is one in which the ovaries of the female are removed. This operation, of course, removes the main objection to the presence of a female in the houeshold, but at the same time, if it is done too early, it may in some way affect the general makeup and mentality of the bitch as she grows older.

A spayed dog is not eligible for showing, and, of course, it cannot be bred. There is no way, once the operation is done, of undoing it.

If a bitch puppy is allowed to develop normally, then, of course, she will have her periods of heat and, as I said earlier, should, in my opinion, be bred from. This is often a very good thing for, in a family where there are children, the birth and bringing up of a litter of puppies can be of tremendous value in the education of the human family, and Collies are wonderful mothers.

Should your choice turn to the male, then there is one thing which can be said against him. The dog, as opposed to the bitch, has a greater desire and tendency to roam, but here again, in the breed you have chosen, this tendency appears to be less great than in many other breeds. It would seem that the Collie is a dog for whom his home, his family and his domestic life are more important than his animal instincts.

Which Collie to Choose

Now that you have decided not only what breed of dog you wish to own, but also what sex your puppy is to be, the moment has come

A Collie is a dog for whom his home, his family, and his domestic life are more important than anything else.

Many people feel that the Shetland Sheepdog is a "bred down in size" version of our beloved Collie. This belief is further strengthened by the fact that so many call the Shetland Sheepdog, or Sheltie, a Miniature Collie. While they may at some time in the distant past have had a common ancestor, they have been distinct and separate breeds for many, many years.

for you to make your final choice. Where are you going to make it? There are numerous alternatives before you; but the best advice that one can be given is to attend a few dog shows first of all, for even in the same breed, type varies from kennel to kennel, and it is up to you to make up your mind which of the different types you yourself prefer. Having come to this decision, arrange to visit a breeder of reputable stock. The Kennel Club of your own country will give you the names of such breeders, or, by visiting the shows, you may well have found them for yourself.

Buying from a Pet Shop

However, if it should so happen that you are situated far from a Collie kennel, your town will undoubtedly have one or more pet shops. These puppy stores are not all reliable but other Collie owners will be able to offer sound advice. It may be that the pet shop of your choice will not have the puppy you want in stock, but the dealer will have greater facilities for obtaining such a puppy than you. A reliable pet shop will have contacts with equally reliable breeding kennels, and if you are truly in earnest about buying a puppy, he may propose an arrangement with such a kennel whereby a puppy can be sent on approval to the shop for you to make your final choice.

Most kennels will not consider sending a puppy on approval to a private home. This is quite understandable. The risk is far too great. The breeder can never be sure whether the unknown prospective purchaser has just lost a dog from disease, nor can he know whether the prospective purchaser will keep the puppy, feed it well for the few hours it is in his care, and send it back promptly if it is

Look at me! Aren't I beautiful?

not wanted. Even a few hours of wrong feeding will harm a very young puppy, and no kennel worth its salt will risk this "on approval". You must not believe, when a kennel refuses to send a puppy for you to see before you make your final decision, that the kennel has something to hide. This is not the case at all.

Buying From a Kennel

As you may prefer to see several puppies before making your choice, quite the best thing to do is to telephone one or more kennels, and find out what they have to offer. Visit them only by appointment, for nothing is more annoying than to arrive and find the gates locked and the owner away, and nothing is more annoying for a kennel owner than to have somebody arrive when he or she is in the middle of feeding or same other chore.

Now let us suppose that you have arrived at a certain kennel. Let us also suppose that there are four or five puppies from which to make your choice. Do take the owner of the kennel into your confidence; tell him exactly what you want. Do you want a puppy with a fabulous temperament just as a pet for you and your children, regardless of how he will look when he grows up; or, just a puppy with which you will not be ashamed to be seen? Or even more, do you want a puppy to be taken into the show ring with the hope of winning a few prizes? Naturally, the price of the degrees of puppy will vary and that is why I say, take the breeder into your confidence. Say just how much you are prepared to spend, and the breeder will then tell you whether, for that sum, you can purchase a puppy of the quality you wish or whether you will need to lower your sights.

Remember too, while you can expect your puppy to be soft and fluffy, his coat will be relatively short, not at all like the magnificent coat of the adult Collie. This will come later, as he matures over a period of years. If the puppy is between three and six months of age he may look downright ugly, gawky and gangly – his legs and neck too long and his coat sparse. This is a perfectly normal part of growing up.

It won't be easy to choose your pet, particularly if you take the family along, because you will undoubtedly see a mass of furry, lovable, adorable babies, each one assuring you that he is the one you want, while each member of your family is probably choosing

While you can expect your puppy to be soft and fluffy, his coat will be relatively short, not at all like the magnificent coat of the adult Collie. This will come later as he matures.

a different one. However, you must steel yourself against the soft-hearted child of the family who picks out the saddest looking puppy of the tribe, and says, "Oh, Daddy, let's have this one. I don't think the others are very kind to him". Probably that puppy is a little shy. He may grow out of it. He may end up as a top dog, but you would be taking a risk and, soft-hearted though the family may be, this is a puppy which should be avoided. But neither should you choose the puppy who throws himself at you first. He may be the out-and-out-extrovert, the kind of puppy who grows up into the wandering dog; or the dog that will go off with anyone regardless of whether he knows them or not, leaving his family abandoned.

Watch the puppies playing together for a while; look for the self-possessed happy one – the one who doesn't get nasty when the others bump into him and knock him over, the one who takes everything in his stride. He will be the one for you, particularly if you have a boisterous human family with which he will have to contend. Avoid the one who retreats when you approach and who will not come towards your outstretched hand. A reliable breeder will quick-

When choosing a puppy, look for the self-possessed happy one – the one who takes everything in his stride. He is the one for you.

ly be able to size up you and your family. If you tell him something of the environment in which the puppy will grow up, where your house is located, the size of it, and so forth, he will help you considerably in picking the right puppy.

Now that you have made what you think is your final choice, pick your puppy up, make sure he is firm, warm and rounded, his eyes bright and his coat clear and shiny. His body should be well covered with flesh; you should not be able to feel his ribs. His eyes should be bright and sparkling, and his ears clean. There should be no spots on his belly, and, of course, there should be no signs of fleas or any other parasites. Occasionally one finds a puppy with an umbilical hernia. This shows itself as a raised spot or bubble in the middle of the abdomen, which, if pressed gently, disappears. It is rare that an umbilical hernia is serious. More often than not it disappears as the puppy grows older, but if you are in doubt, it is wise to have the puppy checked by a veterinarian before you finalize your purchase. If the hernia does not disappear as the puppy grows older, it can be removed by quite a minor operation, but you must, of course, consider the added cost. Avoid a coughing dog or one with yellow mucus at the eyes or nose.

The skin of the puppy should, when pulled up, snap back into place quickly, and not be spongy. With a long-haired breed it is more important to look for patches of possible skin disease; these are noticeable in a short-haired dog, but a fairly close inspection is needed when choosing a Collie puppy. However, it would be most unlikely for a reputable dealer even to offer such a puppy.

An old wives' tale tells us that if a puppy's nose is hot, the puppy is unwell. This is completely untrue. If you are in doubt, take the puppy's temperature. The normal temperature of a dog is 101° to 102.2° F, but frequently with puppies that have been playing, particularly in hot weather, the temperature may rise as high as 103°F. or possibly even more, so this would have no great significance. However, if I were choosing a puppy, and I found one with a temperature higher than normal, I would ask to have it kept in a quiet place for half an hour; at the end of that time the puppy should have a normal temperature. If the temperature remains high and your heart is set on this particular puppy, ask the seller to hold it for a day or two. In that time get a veterinarian to check it, and let the matter rest on his decision.

Choosing a Potential Champion

If you are buying a puppy with which you have hopes of winning in the show ring, or from which you hope to breed future champions, you will, of course, want to obtain the best dog or bitch possible. You will devote much more time to your selection than you would

Champion Coronation Golden Echo. Bred and owned by Isabel Chamberlin, he is shown winning Best of Breed of the Collie Club of Alabama.

for a companion Collie, and, undoubtedly, more money. You will take time to visit dog shows in your area, read the dog magazines to see what leading breeders may be nearby, and you may even enter into correspondence with kennels at a distance, ultimately paying them a visit. In the dog show world, the right Collie can put you several generations ahead of the game, so it is highly important that you choose wisely and well.

Prices

You will have to pay more for the best but the purchase price is little in terms of long-term investment. In a dog show, the difference is worthwhile in terms of proud satisfaction. The serious breeder of show dogs spends time and money on quality stock, stud fees, proper nutrition for mother and puppies, vaccinations, and health care. In addition, he stands behind his stock – you are getting a quality product.

Age

When you buy a show prospect, remember that no breeder can guarantee with any degree of certainty that the cute little ball of fluff which is only six or eight weeks old will turn into an outstanding adult. A wiser investment, if what you want is a show prospect, would be a pup of six to eight months who has already outgrown the awkward stages, so that his future potential may be assessed. Safest of all is the purchase of an adult. Should you decide on a female for breeding, a proven producer of quality puppies need not necessarily be the acme of show dogs herself, but she can help you to produce them.

However, if you are determined to have all the pleasure of raising your puppy from babyhood, do be guided by the advice of its breeder in your selection. No one unfamiliair with the strain can pick a puppy easily at one sitting. In addition, different bloodlines develop differently. The breeder knows his own stock, what to look for and what to avoid, and has been watching the litter develop.

If you want your future show dog to grow up looking like this ideal merle, English Champion Vanity Blue from Valebridge, you must choose your puppy wisely and well.

If you show that you are sincere in your intention to care for and train your puppy properly, and to campaign it in the shows, the conscientious breeder will see to it that his recommendation justifies your trust.

Pedigree

Every purebred dog has a pedigree, which means little unless you know the individuals named on it. When buying a show dog, the show and producing records of the parents and grandparents and, more important, the fact that many show winners have been produced within the family, are what count. Champions many generations back on the pedigree don't necessarily mean much, because since then they have probably had hundreds if not thousands of descendants, perhaps few of them of show quality.

Points in Selection

There are many points to look for in a show prospect. Read this section carefully and re-read it several times before you start looking. Studying different litters will give you some idea of the bare essentials. But the greatest help of all would be to take with you to the breeding kennels a friend who knows all about show-quality Collies.

First, it must be a healthy, well developed puppy. The temperament of the parents and the presence of obviously healthy kennelmates are even more important in selecting a show prospect than when buying a pet.

Color and markings are unimportant, almost immaterial. You may be guided by personal preference, but do not fall for a big white collar alone. A washed-out pale Sable without the face mask, a badly marked Blue or one with two light eyes, a heavily-marked White, or rusty Tricolor will lose out, but markings are of little note compared to overall quality.

Babyhood is not too early for an indication of profuse coat. Choose the puppy with "guard hairs" – long soft hair overlying the puppy fuzz. When you see the pups, the mother will probably be in the midst of shedding, but note if she has the proper harsh, stand-off double coat, with the proper length of furnishings, and the same goes for the sire.

The ears on a puppy should be well set up on the head and tipped forward. They continue to rise all through the dog's life, so a young pup's ears should be well broken. If you have a carrying basket like this one, take it along when picking up your puppy. He will travel in greater comfort.

Males should be masculine, bitches feminine. You should be able to tell which is which just by their overall appearance at any age. In either, however, you want a block head with full, rounded muzzle and well filled-out underjaw. The head should not be too deep through the throat. Snipiness or a pinched-in muzzle is to be avoided at all cost, because the head continues to lengthen and narrow all the time it develops, and the muzzle will never be proportionately greater as an adult than it was a puppy. Eyes should be dark but bright. Beware the pup whose parents have large, round, or yellow eyes. The haw, or inner eyelid, should not be visible. If the eye is small enough its color is not important.

Ears should be set well up on the head and tipped forward. They continue to rise all through the dog's life, so a young pup should have ears well broken. A little help with a moleskin prop or liquid adhesive at five to six months may be necessary to bring them up, but ears which are pricked at an early age will always be a problem.

During teething the ears may go up and down, but they should never be allowed to stay up for more than a single day. Grease them to bring the top over and keep the "break".

Too many Collies lack soundness and elegance. The first is due chiefly to faulty shoulder structure or lack of angulation in the assembly. Look at the parents, for this is a fault which is seen more clearly in the adult. The dog should move freely, without pawing the air in hackney action, or crossing over, although the paws should track closely together, particularly at a rapid trot.

Choose a puppy with arch and length of neck, combined with as short and cobby a body as possible, not shallow or shelly. With his fluffy coat the puppy should look stocky and his legs heavy-boned, although the adult Collie is a dog "without useless timber" and never massive. The tail should be long, reaching at least to the hock or heel, and carried low.

Like begets like, and if you choose carefully, selecting the best that is available from the best stock, you have a good chance of success.

Registration Papers

When buying a purebred puppy, whether from a registered kennel, a private breeder, or a reputable pet shop, you will naturally expect to get a *registered* puppy, so it is necessary to know a little bit about the "papers". When selling a registered dog, the vendor should give you registration papers made out to you in your name at the time the sale is made. If papers are not yet available – as may very well happen because of red tape and regulations – the seller must, at the barest minimum, give you in writing the name and registration numbers of the sire and dam of your puppy, the date of birth, and the name of the breeder. If he cannot provide these, you may very well question the authenticity of your puppy's registration. Have him guarantee in writing that he will provide papers for your puppy.

This may not seem too important at the time of purchase, but you will see later on just how important registration is. Far too many people neglect to secure the papers, feeling that they are only for owners who intend to breed or show their dogs. And then, when the puppy grows up to be a real beauty, they regret overlooking the papers because unless a dog is properly registered with the American

This is a tricolor Collie puppy with his ears propped to help keep them up.

Kennel Club he cannot be entered in an AKC licensed show. Moreover, unless *both* parents are registered, their offspring cannot be registered with the AKC.

Also bear in mind that a pedigree is not a substitute for the registration papers. The AKC will always, for a moderate fee, provide a pedigree once you have the registration papers, but they will not register a dog for you even if you have a pedigree unless you also have the correct registration papers.

Usually what the seller provides is registration application papers. The Kennel Club issues these when the breeder applies for registration of a litter – one blue certificate for each puppy. The breeder fills out the sex, color and the name of the person he sells it to. If you are the purchaser your name will be filled in on the back. If the breeder has sold the puppy to someone else first, then the breeder must make out a gray transfer to that party, and each subsequent purchaser must do the same until the puppy is registered under his own individual name.

To register the puppy, fill in at the top of the blue certificate the name you would like him to have for the rest of his life. A second choice is also necessary in the event that for some reason the first is unacceptable. The person who sold the dog to you will print your name in the proper space and sign it. Sign your name in the space below provided for that purpose (Section B) and send it to the AKC with the proper fee as soon as possible. Later then, if you happen to misplace the papers, you will be able to get duplicates.

Otherwise, if you lose them, you will have to go back to the last registered owner – in most cases the registered breeder – and ask him for duplicates. This is often difficult to do – particularly several years later when the breeder may have moved.

If your puppy has already been individually registered with the AKC, the seller will fill out the transfer on the back and sign it.

The Kennel Clubs in different countries have different rules, and it is as well to familiarize yourself with the local ones before purchasing a puppy. In Britain, for instance, a puppy can be registered by someone *other* than the breeder, and a puppy of unregistered parentage can be registered.

Give some thought to what you are going to do with your puppy when you arrive home. He should have his own bed so that he can learn where to go and rest when he wishes to. He should become accustomed to this right away.

LOUISE VAN DER MEID

There are right and wrong ways to pick up and carry a puppy. He must be held securely and yet comfortably, so that he will enjoy being held, and you can enjoy holding his soft, furry body without his wriggling in discomfort.

V   The New Puppy

Use a little forethought when you go to collect your puppy; put into the car some kind of box in which to take him home. However, if you cannot find a suitable box, probably the breeder will be able to lend you one, and I stress the word "lend" because some breeders do expect to get their boxes back. In the first days of traveling, puppies will sometimes become car-sick, although this is not too often the case with Collies. However, the breeder may give the puppy some kind of tablet to prevent car sickness, and you will know what brand to use on future occasions, if it becomes necessary. It is quite probable that, even if a puppy is sick on his first journey, he will rapidly grow out of it, particularly if, by being given a car-sickness tablet before starting on his next few journeys, he gains confidence and realizes that going in a car does not mean he has to be sick. But, for the sake of all concerned on this first journey, it is wisest to keep him in a box.

Sleeping Quarters

Before setting out to get your puppy, you will, I hope, have given some thought about what you are going to do with him when you arrive home. You should already have decided where and in what he is to sleep. He should have his own box where he knows that he may go and rest when he wishes to, and he should become accustomed to this right away. It will give him a great sense of security. We will assume first that your puppy will be living and sleeping in the house. I suggest he should have a box about 24 inches long, 24 inches high, and some 18 inches wide; the box to be stood on its side so that the entrance naturally is on the dog's level. Across the open end place a board, some 4 inches to 6 inches high, which will keep in any bedding and keep out drafts. This box, you will be surprised to know, will be big enough for him for the rest of his life. An adult Collie can entirely disappear in a box this size. Ideally, the box should be raised 2 inches or 3 inches from the floor.

Handling Your Puppy

Just as there are right and wrong ways to pick up and carry a human baby, so there are right and wrong ways to pick up and carry a puppy. As your Collie will eventually grow into a dog of reasonable size, you do not want him to become a lap dog, and so it is best to pick him up as little as possible; let him learn that a dog's place is on the ground. However, there are times when picking up is essential. The way to do this is to put one hand under the puppy's chest between his hind legs, so that when you raise him from the ground, the whole of his weight is taken on his own bony structure, with no chance of injuring any of his internal organs. When you want to put a puppy back down again, either do it in exactly the same manner, or take him with hands on either side of his shoulders, and place him on the ground with his hind legs first, making sure that they have a firm grip and that he is balanced before you lower his front end.

Carrying your puppy is something else again. Obviously, you

will not want to have both your hands occupied while you are carrying him. So, put his body under your arm, and with his head facing forward, put your hand under his chest with the thumb over his outside elbow, put a couple of fingers under his chest, and your other two fingers around his inner elbow and tuck his rear end under your elbow. This will keep the puppy from wriggling, and you will be much less likely to drop him.

Sleep

There is one thing frequently neglected in the care of the little puppy. It must be fully realized that the young of any species need a great deal of sleep; if you have small children yourself, you know how much sleep they need. Do not expect the puppy to be always awake, alert and ready for a game, and this is particularly true if you have children of various ages, because they will nap at different times and expect the puppy to play with them when they are awake, with the result that the poor puppy gets no sleep at all. This tends to make him snappy, bad-tempered and nervous. He won't eat and will become irritable and for that you really cannot blame him.

Danger!

"Such things shouldn't happen to a dog". This is an expression one hears frequently but it is amazing the things that can and do happen to dogs, particularly to puppies, simply because we have not foreseen such possibilities. Remember, when you bring your puppy home, that he knows nothing of a house, he knows nothing of heat, he knows nothing of fire, so guard him against every possible accident just as you would a baby. The puppy rollicking toward a fire will, of course, be warned by the heat, but it may well be too late and he may burn himself.

Here are two sad stories which may make you more careful. One, a puppy was sold to a young couple who had just married and were about to move. The day the moving men came, the puppy was shut into the kitchen for safety's sake, as this was to be the last room cleared. When the time came to take the things from the kitchen, the puppy was nowhere to be found, yet doors and windows were closed and had been closed all day. What then had happened? Something that no one could have foreseen. The puppy had found a hole

A child, without intending any harm, can throw a hard ball with enough force to injure a dog. It is much safer to use a soft one such as this, and it's lots of fun.

in the casing of the refrigerator mechanism. He had crept in through it, on a voyage of discovery undoubtedly, and had been decapitated by the fan belt.

Another story I know to be true. A puppy was sold to a family where there were several children. One day these children were out in the garden, playing with a hard ball. Pup, of course, joined in. One of the children threw the ball, not intending to harm the puppy at all – but you know what childish aim is. The puppy was hit at the base of the skull and dropped down dead on the spot.

Such are the hazards for which to be prepared. It is not possible to foresee them all, but one must always try to anticipate them. Never leave a broom standing on end, for instance. It is so easy for the puppy to knock it over, and have it fall on him. Do not leave a tablecloth dangling over the edge of the table where it will tempt the puppy to pull it; even if he does not injure himself this time, he won't do a great deal of good to the meal that is on the table. Think of the door or gate blowing in the wind. I know of a puppy who had his head crushed flat by a garage door which blew closed when he was exploring the hinge end of that door. I know of another whose neck was broken when a refrigerator door was slammed shut. And don't leave live electric wires where he may chew them! I could tell you many stories but perhaps these are enough to alert you to some of the things that can happen to a dog, especially during the early months of his life.

Feeding Your Puppy

If you purchase your puppy from a reliable source you will be given a diet sheet, telling you what he has been eating, and listing the changes that should be made in his diet during the coming few weeks. Remember that from now on the responsibility for your puppy's future is yours, and yours alone, and much of this future depends upon how you feed him. Your puppy should receive at least

A very young puppy should receive at least four, preferably five meals daily. These can be reduced in number as he matures.

TOM CARAVAGLIA

four, preferably five meals daily, and these meals must constitute a balanced diet. We will not go into details here of what a balanced diet is because this is described in detail in Chapter VIII.

Your puppy should continue to have his five meals daily until he is about twelve weeks old; then the meals may be reduced to four in number, but increased slightly in size. This increase applies particularly to his two meat meals. The "four meals" daily routine can be continued as long as the puppy is willing to eat as frequently as this, particularly in the winter months, but he could certainly be fed four meals a day until he has arrived at the age of six months. At this age the meals can be cut to three. These should be continued as long as the puppy is teething; he will finish his teething at seven to nine months, although this varies considerably from individual to individual.

When he has completed teething, his meals may be cut to twice daily and these two adult meals should be given to him for the rest of his life. Full details will be found in Chapter VIII.

For some weeks to come, all food should be given with the chill off, for it is extremely detrimental to give stone cold food to a young puppy.

For his breakfast the puppy should have milk, probably about half a pint, with dog meal, or cereals, plus any essential vitamins in which his diet may be lacking.

Some people believe that at mid-morning he should receive a meat meal – preferably raw meat. He will want at least eight ounces of meat at each of his meat meals. In the early afternoon he will be glad to have a bowl of milk with a puppy biscuit to chew, and then late afternoon a further meat meal, similar to that of mid-morning. At bedtime he can have a bowl of meal or kibble, scalded with boiling beef stock, and allowed to cool to body heat before feeding.

Nutritional experts, those people who formulate commercial dry type dog foods, know that meat and milk need not necessarily be fed in fresh form. They recommend feeding a complete dry type food (to which liquid is added) at every meal. They contend that variety is not necessary. Their studies show that puppies grow more rapidly and as soundly in every way when fed their prepared foods as do those fed raw meats and fresh milk with variety in their diets.

It is extremely difficult to indicate the quantity to feed, because this varies so much from puppy to puppy; you are the only one

Collies are popular all around the world. This is a Swedish champion blue merle. The ribbons on his leash are awards won in previous shows.

who can tell just how much your puppy needs. Gradually increase the size of each meal, giving him all he will clean up within five minutes. If you want your puppy to have a hard biscuit to chew, give it to him at bedtime.

All the time he is growing up, it is perfectly safe and very good to give him raw bones, but I do stress *raw*, and that they should be *big* bones, ones he will be unable to splinter. Marrow bones will give him endless fun, because he will be able to lick and pull at the marrow, although he cannot splinter the actual bone. He must always have water. Fresh water twice a day should be your rule. Never leave your puppy without fresh water to drink.

Continue then with this routine, increasing the quantity and decreasing the number of meals, so that by the time the puppy is six months old he will be down to three a day.

The First Night Home

Having arrived home with your puppy, remember do, that this is a tremendous change for him. He is very young, and does not as yet understand a great deal. He may have been away from his mother before, but probably never from his brothers and sisters. He will be both lonely and bewildered so you must be extremely patient and understanding, for this is a time when his whole character may be

Collies, bred as they are for herding, instinctively look after young and helpless creatures. They are gentle, tender and protective.

SALLY ANNE THOMPSON

made or marred for the future. He must learn quickly to depend on you, and this will come easily if he is met with sympathy.

Before bringing him home, decide where you want him to sleep and have his bed ready. If he has been upset on the journey, he will probably be tired when he gets home, so it is best to offer him only a drink of water and to put him into his bed and let him sleep for a while if he will.

As I said earlier, a box makes a suitable bed. If you wish, during the early days until he is really sure that the box is his very own, it can have a wire front on it to keep him shut in until he is thoroughly accustomed to his new house.

An hour or two after arriving, he may be given a meal – which one will depend entirely upon the time of day you bring him home. It is wise, however, to arrange to give him his last meal, say, about an hour before you yourself are ready to go to bed, so that he may eat it, be given his last run, and be settled in bed with a chance to accustom himself to his surroundings before you leave him. At any rate, do not expect your puppy to lie quietly in his bed if there is a lot of movement still going on in the house. If he can hear you talking, if he can hear the television or the radio, he will obviously want to be with you, and he will squeal and cry unless he is.

When you do go to bed and all is quiet, give him a little while to quiet down. If he does not, it is probably because he misses the warmth and companionship of his littermates and so he calls to let them know where he is. If he cries unhappily and seems unable to settle down, go to him, but do not give in to him. Don't for the sake of peace take him to sleep in your own bed; once you do this, it will be almost impossible to break him of the habit later on. One of the best ways to quiet him is to give him a little warmth in his bed so that he will think he still has a brother or sister with him. A soft wooly toy to cuddle up to may well be sufficient answer; but if it is winter and cold, it will help considerably if you fill a hot water bottle (cover it with a blanket so there is no chance of the puppy scalding himself) and put it under the paper or other bedding that you have given your puppy, so that he can snuggle up to it and feel warm and comforted.

Although, obviously, you will not want to be kept awake all night by your puppy's squealing, do be kind; do not be cross with him that first night for he needs much understanding. However, I may have painted too gloomy a picture of the first night home, for out of the

If you have other pets in your household, introduce the new puppy to them so that they will become firm friends.

hundreds of puppies I have parted with over the years, many, many times have I been told, "He has been good as gold; there has not been a sound out of him – not even that first night!" Remember! A puppy soon outgrows his night crying so be patient but be firm, and it will end surprisingly soon.

If your puppy is sleeping in the house, there is no reason why he cannot be left in a cage or pen all night. This will keep him from waking and becoming bored, getting out and finding wild games to play, and things to chew, such as the corner of the carpet! Also, for reasons which I explain later, the use of a cage or pen will be of great help when it comes to his housebreaking.

Many puppies enter a home as Christmas gifts. There is nothing wrong with this, provided the family is warned in advance, and proper preparations for receiving the newcomer are made.

VI Teaching Your Puppy to Behave

Housebreaking

The first thing you will want to teach your puppy is to be clean in the house. With a Collie this takes very little doing – they are instinctively clean as a breed, and housebreaking presents few problems. If you live in an apartment or a house with no yard, then obviously you must paper train your puppy. In any other circumstances, and with a dog the size of the Collie, paper training cannot really be recommended. However, if there is no alternative, this is what you should do. Put his bed into an enclosed corner of the room – placing the whole thing inside a child's play-pen is even better.

The enclosed area of floor should then be covered entirely with newspaper, and it should be left so until the puppy has shown you which area he prefers using. When you have discovered this, remove the newspaper from all other areas. You will soon find that when he is enclosed in this space, he will always use that portion of newspaper. But do not forget when you let him out to play always to give him access to his "comfort-station".

If at all possible, however, do not paper train your puppy; instead, teach him from the very beginning to go outside. To do this, pick him up the moment he wakes up – every single time he wakes up – and put him out. Put him out as soon as he has had a meal. Put him out when he has finished playing and is about to drop off to sleep. Each time go with him, so that when he has relieved himself you are on hand to praise him; this will help him to understand much more quickly what he is supposed to do. If he makes a mistake in the house, of course he must be scolded, but gently and firmly; he should not have his nose rubbed in it, nor should he be beaten. The Collie is so sensitive to moods that a little scolding is all that is required.

Set up a regular routine of taking or letting your puppy out, because dogs, it seems, have a built-in clock, and they quickly know that the time to do a certain thing has come around again; if you set out, say, a regular three-hourly program during the day your puppy will very quickly become accustomed to it and get the idea of answering his calls of nature outside. In a very few days you will find him going to the door and asking to be let out. It is up to you to see that he is let out the moment he asks, for if not, and he makes a mistake, you have nobody but yourself to blame and must surely never scold the puppy.

When you take him out, go to some fairly distant spot, for he will quickly associate this spot with what he has to do, and later when he is let out alone, he will go to it. If you just take him outside the back door, again you can blame no one but yourself if forever after there is always a little pile outside your door. It is natural for a puppy to keep his sleeping quarters clean; it was for this reason I said earlier that you might well enclose your puppy inside his sleeping box at night. But do this only if the first person in the house to awake goes at once to the box, gets the puppy out, and puts him outside. This is the quickest way I know to night housetrain a puppy. This, however, is not recommended if you are one of the "early to bed and late to rise" brigade, because you really cannot expect a puppy to wait for much more than six hours. It would be bad for him if he did. If he is forced by nature to dirty his box during a prolonged confinement, it could become a bad habit.

If it was at first necessary to train your puppy to paper and you now wish to train him to go outdoors, he will have to go through a short transitional period. Gradually move the paper a little nearer the door each day, until finally the time comes to place it outside the back door, firmly anchored with stones. Take your puppy to this paper and he will quickly realize that this is what he is used to using. Gradually reduce the paper until there is none left at all.

Regular Routine

Housebreaking is a matter of regular routine. A dog's most urgent calls of nature will come after each meal and as soon as he wakes in the morning. This then should set your routine – you will know when and what to expect. You must go about it calmly, patiently, and with the greatest possible regularity.

When, as will happen, the puppy does make a mistake, take him at once to the scene of his crime. He must be shown what he has done and corrected very firmly. By firm correction, however, I do not mean a beating; he must only be scolded. It is incredible that even today we still find people with the idea that if a puppy makes a mistake, he should have his nose rubbed in it. This is unmitigated cruelty. The puppy is afraid, first from the rough handling; second, because he has no idea why this revolting thing is happening to him, and when released he will probably rush off and hide out of sheer terror. Rather, take your puppy to the scene of the crime, scold him firmly but gently, and then either take him to the paper that he should have used, or put him out the door, according to his training.

It is not possible to say just how long it takes to housebreak a dog, because it varies from animal to animal. With a fit, healthy puppy it should only be a matter of days, at the most a week. But I stress "fit, healthy" because all evacuation is controlled by muscles, and the puppy whose muscles are not in really fit condition will take longer to break than one who is absolutely fit. This, too, is another reason for not rubbing the puppy's nose in his mess because fright engenders weakness, and all you'll do is end up with a puppy unable to contain himself because his excretory muscles have been weakened. Never physically chastise a young Collie puppy; they are so sensitive that a good shaming with your voice is all that is required. Only his feelings will be hurt, and you will end up with a puppy with faith and trust in you and which you will never achieve if you physically manhandle him.

Urinary Behavior

Young puppies of both sexes squat to urinate. With the female this attitude persists through life, but with the male it changes at puberty. As they mature sexually, males begin to lift a hind leg and direct their urine against some object – the long-suffering tree and fire hydrant, for instance. At this time too, they begin to urinate more frequently, and to "hold back", expelling only a little urine at a time and distributing it over a wide area, thus leaving a trail wherever they go. This serves to mark the boundary of the individual dog's territory. In the wild stage, it served to inform any stray animal that "this land is mine".

Males can differentiate between the odor of masculine and feminine urine; they can also detect whether or not the female is in heat. Sometimes an old bitch or one that has been spayed will urinate like a male.

Unfortunately, the male who disposes of his urine in small doses over a wide area is often responsible for ruining valuable shrubs, soiling cars, store fronts and even bystanders' legs. To minimize the male's opportunities for this unpleasantness, you can do little except anticipate the raising of his leg. A good plan is to train him to use one or two spots where his urination can cause no offense. Once he has adopted such places he will be inclined to save up for them.

Discipline

A puppy must always be corrected at the moment he commits his "crime". You can't expect him to understand, if you come home and find he has eaten the toes of your slippers, why he is being spanked for something that he did hours ago. If something like this does happen, blame yourself for leaving your slippers out and never chastise him unless you can catch him in the act of misbehaving. Then and then alone can you expect him to understand.

I think it is necessary to draw a line between what is to be considered real naughtiness that must be punished, and what is only puppy play. For example, I once saw a woman breeder step into a room full of puppies. The puppies rushed up to play and one undid her shoe laces; I saw that poor little puppy spanked for this. No, if you cannot bear to have a puppy untie your shoe laces, you ought not to breed dogs.

Training a puppy, or an adult dog for that matter, is also a training of one's self. It demands a great deal of self-discipline, kindness, control, and not the slightest loss of temper. Having once decided that a puppy is to be corrected for doing a certain thing, you must always correct him for that same thing. It is no good telling him he is naughty for chewing the corner of the carpet today, and laughing at him when he does it tomorrow. It will get you nowhere and completely destroy the puppy's discipline.

Chewing

The only way to teach a puppy that he must not chew things is to watch and correct him constantly. Once again, for correction, it is only necessary to scold, not physically chastise. A great deal can be accomplished by giving your puppy his own toys, with which he will quickly learn to play. These toys should be of the kind that cannot do him harm – a large solid ball, a strong solid rubber bone, and fresh marrow bones are all things that cannot harm him and with which he can have lots of fun.

Your puppy will, particularly during teething time, have a tendency to chew, and it is up to you not to let it become a habit. It is only a means of play, and your puppy should be taught quite early that there are things with which he may play, and things which he may not. Any wrong kind of chewing must be corrected immediately. It is up to you just how much your puppy gets away with.

He must be taught what is correct, and what is incorrect, and he must be taught this by the firm use of the word "No."

If you come across him chewing something he should not, don't lose your temper and scold him. Simply say "No", give him one of his own toys, let him go on chewing and in this way he will rapidly

You must establish rapport with your dog, and what better way to do so than by sharing a meal. Actually, the author does not recommend feeding the dog from your own mouth. But boys will be boys and the relationship between a boy and his dog often transcends everything else.

learn the difference between what he may and may not use his teeth on.

Some puppies will learn this quickly; others are more obtuse. It is up to you to be consistent but, at the same time, do not leave too many temptations in his way. If you must go out and leave him on his own, either put him in a pen or kennel, if he has one, or in a room where there is nothing to chew except his own toys. Think this out for yourself. It is first a question of common sense and, second, of perseverance.

Furniture-Breaking

Housebreaking is, of course, your pup's first lesson and by now you should be well on your way with that. Furniture-breaking can go along with it; that is, if you want to keep your pup off beds, chairs and sofas. Some people don't care, or they don't care until it's difficult to break the grown dog of this bad habit.

Naturally your pup loves the easy life. He thinks that a comfortable chair or sofa is meant for him too, when he sees how much you enjoy it. He's intrigued too by that interesting scent you leave behind. It's up to you to teach him his proper place.

First of all, if he has a comfortable spot of his own, he'll be less likely to want yours. A stern "No" emphasized with the crack of a rolled-up newspaper will point out his error. Or, if a newspaper isn't at hand at the critical moment, toss an old book or magazine at his side. Don't hit him – startle him! Let him think it's a bolt from the blue.

He'll catch on quickly if you and every member of the family keep at it. But that's the trick – keeping at it. Being permissive one time and forbidding the next will get you nowhere. Dog repellant sprays are useful for this too. They smell bad to him but not to you and are harmless when instructions are followed.

Other devices include setting mouse traps on a forbidden spot so that when he jumps up they will snap and startle him. Balancing a metal tray of empty cans on the arm of a chair or sofa sometimes works. When he jumps, the tray falls on the floor with a noisy clatter. Still another idea is a tackboard; take a square of cardboard a little smaller than the seat of the chair; push half a dozen thumbtacks through it, and place it, points up, on the chair, hiding it with a remnant of cloth. Ouch! He won't jump on that chair more than twice!

Jumping Up on People

When you have been away for a while your dog will obviously be delighted to see you upon your return, and in greeting he will probably try to jump on you. This is something which must be corrected from the very beginning. It is an extremely bad habit, and one which can be thoroughly embarrassing, particularly when he does it to visitors. This is one trait that can be easily broken provided you start early. Never let him get away with it. The very first time that he does it, raise your leg with the knee bent, and as he jumps, bump him on the chest with your knee. This will almost certainly throw him off balance. If this fails, you can take a step towards him as he jumps at you, and gently, but not too gently, stand on the toes of his back foot – he will quickly learn to associate the little touch of pain with jumping up.

Do remember, though, that you must be consistent. He cannot tell the difference between your good clothes and your workaday ones; so don't let him get away with it today because you have been working in the garden, and scold him tomorrow if he jumps up just as you are coming back from a wedding. Do not blame him if he does.

While you are teaching him this, it is essential that you have the help of your family, as well as any visitors, because they too can give the necessary correction when the dog jumps on them. Be careful, however, not to discourage his greeting completely! Otherwise his

It can be embarassing enough when a puppy jumps up on you, but such behavior is inexcusable in an adult. Gently step on the toes of his back foot as he rears up, and he will quickly learn to associate the little touch of pain with jumping up.

TOM CARAVAGLIA

feelings will be hurt. As soon as all four feet are back on the ground, make a great fuss over him and tell him you are just as pleased to see him as he is to see you.

Biting

Growling and biting are serious and objectionable faults in dogs. They can be cured with simple little lessons which can be given to puppies from the time they are weaned. Growling at the food dish is probably the first bad habit that a puppy gets. And he usually starts by growling at his littermates. He must be taught, however, not to resent his owners.

Most people find that this growling at the food dish has not been cured by the breeder, and so they have to take over. You do this by reaching down to interfere with the puppy's feeding. When he growls, you say "No", grab him by the tail and jerk him away from the food dish, almost rolling him across the floor. He will be startled and surprised by this sudden action.

While you have his attention, caution him, and then let him return to his food. Or, you may give the stern "No" while flicking his nose with your middle finger and thumb.

In either case, the puppy should learn that he must not growl at or try to bite members of the family, and that it remains for you to say when he can eat. The lesson is not hard to teach, but it requires repetition a time or two at each meal until trials show you that the puppy accepts this as one of the "house rules".

All puppies like to roughhouse. But puppies soon bite too hard, and their teeth are very sharp. They also tend to get angry. Your procedure is to play with your puppy until he does get angry and bites too hard. Then you must scold him; and perhaps even punish him, saying "no bite!" several times.

He must learn not to go too far in play, and that he can never growl at or bite a human being. You'll be amazed at how quickly he'll learn this, if you arrange lessons so that he gets one or two a day.

Don't Steal

Some dogs are honest and some are not. Teach yours that the first rule of dog etiquette is not to steal from the table. You can do this by scolding him whenever he shows any interest in food on the table. If he persists then deliberately place food near the table edge with set mouse traps in front of it. Make your "plant" in such a way that the dog will spring the traps before he can reach the food. One or two lessons like this will usually do the trick and you won't have to worry about a breach of good manners again.

Outdoor Manners

Inside the house, your dog's behavior can be whatever you are willing to put up with. But once he's outside, you have a responsibility to the community. Don't let your dog become the neighborhood pest.

Speak to go Out

Some dogs seem to do this almost automatically; others have to be taught. Put your dog inside the door while you step outside. He'll want to join you. Open the door a crack. Command "Speak" in an excited voice, even making a barking noise – anything to get the dog excited. Repeat again and again and all of a sudden, your dog will let out a bark. Instantly open the front door and praise him lavishly. Practice doing this from inside as well as out, so that the dog learns to bark for passage either way.

Yard Breaking

Teach your dog to use only a certain portion of your own yard – behind or beside the garage, or out behind the shrubbery. You can do this by placing some of his droppings there, and then take him to that spot when you know it is necessary. When he relieves himself there, praise him.

Meanwhile, spray any other yard spot he has used previously with a good commercial deodorant. The smell will keep your dog away from those areas, and he will start using the area you prefer.

If you fence the area you have selected, you can leave your dog there for an hour or so at regular times each day.

To keep this area clean, droppings should be disposed of regularly. They can be placed in the street sewer or used in your garden as manure. Various scoop-type gadgets are sold which make it easy to pick up and dispose of the droppings.

Running Away

If, during training for the previous lesson, the dog decides to run away, it will be necessary for you to catch and punish him, then to send him home. However, never call the dog to you and then punish him. This will make him hesitate to come to you the next time you call. Punish him only when you have to go after and catch him. After you have hauled the dog back into your yard, you can praise him so that he'll know he's a good dog when he's in his own yard.

Digging Holes

Dogs often dig holes because of sheer boredom. Occasionally they'll dig just for exercise, but it all stems from an age-old habit of digging for moles, chipmunks, or other game. You can keep your dog from digging again in a hole by placing two or three set traps in the hole. The hole can also be filled with crumpled up chicken wire, well pegged down. Dogs don't like to dig against wire. You can also fill the hole with large stones which he can't move.

The dog will probably dig another hole. But if you repeat the above corrective procedures he'll soon get discouraged.

Sometimes dogs dig holes in very hot weather in order to lie in the cool ground. When this is the cause, bring the dog into the house.

Meet the Mailman

Properly brought up pups just don't get the idea that it's permissible to bite the mailman or meter reader. Highly nervous dogs, dogs that are kept tied up for long periods, and basically shy dogs who attack out of fear may attempt to bite these men or other strangers.

You should introduce your dog to mailmen and meter readers. These men should be encouraged to greet the dog warmly, giving him a chance to smell and investigate them thoroughly. Ask them to call the dog by name and greet him with praise and petting each time they come, until they are accepted as friends.

Do not, however, let them offer the dog a treat. Dogs should never be permitted to accept food from strangers. It is a good idea to learn when these calls are made and, if possible, bring the dog into the house ahead of time. You can thus reassure your dog that all is well.

Awareness of Vehicles

In these days of heavy traffic, one rarely finds a dog who is a car chaser, if for no other reason than that the moment he starts to chase, he almost certainly dies a sudden death; but it is wise to make your dog completely aware of cars and of their danger. If he goes travelling with you a great deal, he will usually rush to the car, wanting to get in and ride happily. Unfortunately, this may lead him to think that he can do the same thing with other people's cars, even when they are moving.

To teach him the danger, you will need the help of a car driver. Find a quiet road, or even a fairly flat field, and go into it with your dog on a long lead or rope. Your helper will drive slowly, and since he is aware of what you are doing, the dog runs no risk. When he attempts to rush at the car, jerk him back and scold him severely. If this is not enough, have another friend ride in the car. Let

English Champion Anton Vicar of Bray at 2½ years. He excels in richness of color.

the dog approach until he is almost at the car door. The passenger should then throw something, preferably a cup of water, into the dog's face; this will quickly teach him not to approach cars from the side.

To teach him the dangers of cars head-on is equally simple. Again, put him on the long lead and let him run about while the the car is being driven slowly through the field. If he makes no attempt to approach the car, ask the driver to follow the dog until he can just bump the dog gently with the bumpers or the tire – not enough, of course, to hurt him, just enough to frighten him.

If, despite this, he still has a tendency to chase cars, again put him on the long line, let him get going, and just as he comes to the end of the rope, call "No" sharply, jerking him up so short that he falls off his feet. This treatment, administered once or twice, will quickly teach him not to chase automobiles.

The Barking Dog

Dogs by nature will bark, but they must not be allowed to bark unnecessarily. If your dog barks when somebody knocks on the door, or rings the door bell, do not consider it unnecessary. It may well be that you have not heard the summons yourself, and the dog can be of help. However, if you go out, and on your return are met with neighbors because your dog has barked non-stop while you were gone, then, obviously, he has been barking unnecessarily.

If the dog appears to be barking for no reason, go to him and, gently tapping his muzzle with your finger, command him "Quiet". If this does not have any effect, hold his muzzle in your hand, and again give the command. This is usually sufficient. However, if you are blessed with a dog that likes the sound of his own voice, more severe measures must be taken. If you can correct him from a distance, good! If you are a straight shot, throw something at him, something that will make a lot of noise, but won't hurt him – for instance, a light aluminum alloy chain, or two or three empty cans tied together. This should quickly show him that he is making a grave mistake. As you throw, also use the word "Quiet" in a very firm and clipped tone. A few repetitions of this ought to have the desired effect, but if he is unexpectedly stubborn, try throwing a glass of water in his face. It works better, however, if you can correct a noisy dog from a distance.

Once a dog has learned what the word "Quiet" means, he will almost always be quiet as long as you are with him, but what happens the minute your back is turned? To overcome barking while you are gone, you must pretend that you are going away. Get dressed as if to go out, and be quite sure in your own mind that you are going out, otherwise, the dog will sense that this is just a play. Leave your dog in his usual place and go out of the house. Walk a little distance away, return very quietly and wait. The moment you hear him start to bark, open the door quickly – if he is behind it and gets hit, so much the better – and immediately spank him on the muzzle, preferably with a folded newspaper which you will be holding just for this purpose. Keep repeating that word "Quiet", of course. You will probably have to do this over and over again, but it is well worth it. You will be able to cure him in just one day if you make up your mind that by that evening you are going to have a quiet dog. But you must keep at it, so schedule a period when you have several hours to spare. It is no good leaving the job half done.

Test him then by going out for short periods, hoping that you will return to a silent dog. If you do, gradually extend the length of time until you are absolutely certain that he is trustworthy in your absence. However, if you return and find him barking, this is the moment once again to censure him severely, so that he will come to understand that when you are not there he must be quiet.

Another training device is the muzzle. Do not, of course, except as a very last resort, leave the dog muzzled when you go away. (He can howl, whine, if not bark, even then). Shut the dog in a small room. When he begins to bark go into the room and put his muzzle on him. Leave, shutting the door behind you, and let him remain muzzled for from thirty minutes to an hour. Return, remove the muzzle, and hang it on the door at a spot where the dog can see, but not reach it. Go away and wait for the dog to start barking again. Return, take the muzzle down, and put it back on the dog. Repeat until the dog realizes that he will be muzzled if he doesn't remain quiet when left alone.

Obedience training can help a lot because it makes the dog understand that he must obey on command. When he is well trained in obedience he will stop barking when ordered to, no matter what the occasion, when the doorbell rings, when a visitor approaches, or when about to be left behind.

This training is discussed in Chapter IX.

Puppy Walking

Teaching a puppy to walk on leash is not difficult. First get him used to his new collar by letting him wear it around the house for a little while each day, gradually lengthening the periods until he thinks no more about it. Then tie a short streamer of rag to it – or an old necktie – and let him drag that around. He will tug at it but before long he will get used to the idea of having something dangling from his neck.

Next substitute a short leash for the trailing rag. Let him drag this around the house – under supervision, of course, because he is likely to chew the leather or catch the loop on some protruding object which could choke him. The next step is to parade him around the house (and yard, if you have one) on the leash, but letting him lead and coaxing him along! When he's used to this, take him on the sidewalk for his first venture. Call him to your left side and start walking. He will quickly discover that it is useless to struggle and more comfortable to stay close enough to keep the leash slack. When he does walk quietly by your side, praise him extravagantly, and stroke his muzzle.

Come When Called

If from puppyhood he associates his name with something pleasant, he'll come when called – usually. But there will be times, especially outdoors, when something else will demand his attention and he'll be more interested in that than in you. He must learn to come when he hears his name no matter what his own preference is.

Take your pup outside to an area that is free from any obstruction that could entangle a leash. Attach either a 20-foot training leash to his chain slip collar, or a length of light (quarter-inch) sash cord. Allow him to romp around, getting further and further away from you. When his attention is centered elsewhere, call him cheerfully by name and invite (not command) him to come. If he responds, caress him with praise and slip him a reward. If he does not return immediately, put more sternness in your voice, make it a command, wait only a moment for response and then give the line a sharp jerk – not to choke but to startle him. If he still doesn't react, keep repeating the order sternly as you slowly shorten the line with quick jerks until he is at your side. Now, even though he has returned reluctantly, praise and reward him, and then let him resume play. Now again, when his attention is attracted elsewhere, repeat the exercise, and keep repeating it for about fifteen minutes.

When, after a number of lessons, he responds more or less regularly, try it without the leash. If, however, his response is unsatisfactory give him the additional controlled training and try again.

Owning a Collie is a richly rewarding experience. When you understand the ways of a Collie, and the proper ways of training and caring for him, you will be repaid with the pride of owning the best of all dogs.

There are two schools of thought on whether Collies will grow better coats if kept indoors or out. This is English Champion Pattingham Playbox. He was raised outdoors and he certainly has a magnificent coat. In addition, he has the ideal pigmentation for tricolor.

VII   Kennelling

It is up to you to decide where you want your dog to sleep and where he is to spend most of his time. If you want him as a watchdog, it is probably best to keep him in the house at night. I can't help but think it infinitely preferable for a Collie when he grows up to have some place which is all his own outside. For this purpose I would suggest a kennel building approximately 6 feet by 4 feet, and high enough for you to stand up in comfortably. The building should have a wooden floor, but its framing can be wood, brick or whatever you prefer. It can be peaked roof or lean-to. It all depends on where you want to place it, and what the facilities are in your own yard.

The kennel should be inside a run, the size depends upon the circumstance. If you have a bitch, and think that in the future you may wish to raise a litter, make the run big enough so that there is room for her puppies. A run of, say, 12 feet by 20 feet should be ample; what the base is, I leave to you. Grass is suitable for a puppy run, but it will not stand up to a great deal of pounding from the adult dog, so it might be better to have either a concrete run, a brick run, or a run of sand. It is only a question of which is the easiest for you and which is the most economical. Concrete and brick must be hosed daily, grass is good on the dog's feet but difficult to remove stools from. Sand is probably the best.

A Box Makes a Bed

If your intention is to keep more than one dog, an outdoor kennel and run is essential because there are times when you will not want two or three fairly large dogs ranging through your house, and other times when it will be necessary to separate the dogs from each other.

The kennel building should be light and airy, but free from drafts. The measurements of 6 feet by 4 feet are the *minimum* measurements suitable for a Collie. The kennel can, of course, be a great deal larger, as circumstances and your purse permit. Any outdoor kennel should have either a box in which the dog can sleep, or a raised bed. The bed can be of wood, and need only be raised three inches from the floor. It should have an edge all round it to retain the straw or shavings used for bedding. The box is perhaps best, because I find that a Collie likes to disappear into what he may think of as a "cave" and to hide there if he so wishes. Furthermore, a box is completely draft free if raised a little from the ground. In excessively cold weather a burlap sack or a blanket can be hung over the opening so that the dog may come and go at will, but some of the body heat which he has generated will still be there when he returns.

There are two schools of thought on whether Collies will grow better coats if kept indoors or out. Some say that the warmth of the house prevents a Collie from growing a good coat. Others say that the cold outdoors prevents him growing a thick coat, because he must utilize his food to generate heat within his own body, and has none to spare for making a coat. So it is rather a question of "You pays your money and you takes your choice." As for me, I think that growth of coat depends much more upon the dryness or humidity of the atmosphere, and diet, than it does on actual heat and cold, but more of this in a later chapter.

Many people like to leave their dog free all night. If you are one of them, then a run is, of course, essential. If you have a kennel and a run of the measurements I have given, you have adequate space for your dog – leave the kennel door open all night, and let him come and go as he wishes.

How to fence your run may be your next question. The ideal, of course, is chain link with metal supports, but this is costly, and there are other alternatives to consider, according to the amount you want to spend. Instead of metal posts, wooden, particularly cedar, ones can be used, but wood other than cedar will not last very long. Other types of fencing can be used – ordinary heavy two inch wire-mesh, for instance, called fox farm netting, but it won't last as long as chain link. Other options are sheep fencing, or what is known as universal fencing. However, I have never found these adequate to keep in a baby puppy. It can get out through a very small space, so you should never use wire mesh larger than two-inches. If you prefer to save money by using pig wire, the only thing to do is to interline it with an ordinary two inch mesh chicken wire. This will be cheaper in the end than chain link, but I really do not advise it because the life of chicken wire is short unless you live far away from salt sea air.

The height of the run is your next decision. It should certainly not be less than six feet high; because a mature Collie can easily scale six feet. Some of them can even leap it. If yours grows into a particularly athletic specimen and you find that he is still able to get over a six-foot fence, add about a foot of fencing to the top of the fence and turn inward: this will stop him from climbing or scaling.

The dimensions which I have given for the kennel, at least in regard to height, may seem unnecessary, but if at any time your dog is sick or you have a bitch with puppies, you will constantly bless the day when you decided to build a little house in which you yourself could stand up. For me, there is nothing more tiring than having to tend a dog or puppies when you are bent double. The kennel should, of course, have a glass window which can be opened for ventilation, with the inner side wired over so that the dog cannot get at and break the glass. It is also of great help to make an inner wire door, so that if you so wish, the outer door can be left, with-out letting the dog or puppies out. In bad weather this is a very great help. Whether or not to build a pop hole so that the dog can come and go as he wishes is up to you. On the whole, I find that for Collies pop holes are not really necessary.

A house of these dimensions will easily give room to at least two adult Collies, so look to the future. Though it may look far too big for one small eight-week old puppy, you will be saving money in the long run should you decide to expand your family.

If you decide that your puppy is to sleep in his kennel from the very first night, use the approach that I discussed in Chapter V. But don't think because you have put him in a kennel where you cannot hear him, that he is not crying. If he is going to be unhappy, he will probably be even more unhappy in the kennel, so better give him the creature comforts that I have already suggested. If the weather is really cold, it may be necessary to shut him into his box for the first few nights, so that he cannot come out, get bewildered, and not find his way back, or hide between the box and the wall of the kennel. This is something that frequently happens. The puppy becomes chilled, and you have trouble on your hands. After a few nights of being shut in his box, things will be different; if he comes out, he will easily find his way back because he will want to be where it is warm and comfortable.

Indoor Kennel

Most dog books, including this one, discuss the care and maintenance of dogs in outside kennels, but few point out the advantages of an indoor kennel. This writer recommends one highly.

It can be as simple as a wooden grocery box (or one of heavy cardboard) with a hinged, lockable door and with ventilation holes cut into it. Or it can be an elaborate custom-made doghouse set up in the corner of a large play-pen. It can be four discarded window screens hinged together at the corners, with a fifth screen forming a lid if one is necessary. A corner of a little used room can be fenced off with hardware cloth. In an emergency, a card table turned upside down with wire netting wrapped around its legs will do.

Some owners use the commercial dog crates in which kennels and

I've got a secret! ▶

SALLY ANNE THOMPSON

97

handlers ship dogs to and from new homes and dog shows. These can be purchased in the larger pet shops. While there may be those who will dispute me on this, I think the purchase of a cage or pen for a new puppy is as wise an investment as buying a fancy bed.

Whatever you use, the basic requirements are a fenced off area with a pad or blanket for a bed at one end and a spread of newspapers at the other. When soiled, they can be rolled up and easily disposed of. Provision should also be made for a bowl of fresh water which cannot be tipped over.

The new puppy should be introduced to this, his own "bedroom," as soon as you bring him home. He will quickly come to regard it as his own territory – and owning such a terrain is instinctive to all dogs. If he learns to stay contentedly inside it while he is very young, he will form a lifetime habit of doing so. It will pay off in many ways. For instance, you may have guests who do not like dogs. Towser can be put away. You may want to go out and not give him the run of the house. Again, Towser can be shut inside. You'll have less trouble keeping him off furniture; there'll be less hair to pick up from rugs and chairs. He'll have less opportunity for chewing. When he misbehaves, he can be put "in the doghouse". And when it comes to housebreaking, there is no better training help.

Sometimes, to get a puppy used to such a home, it helps to keep a piece of his master's discarded (unlaundered) clothing in the pen for him to cuddle up to. Its reassuring odor will comfort him, especially the first few nights.

This is not to say that the puppy should be confined to the pen for long periods of time. When someone is around to supervise his activities, he can be let out frequently, and as he gets older and learns not to misbehave and to perform his natural functions where he is supposed to, he can be allowed to enter and leave the pen at will.

The command "Bed!" or "Go to bed" should be taught early. Say "Bed" and point. If the puppy does not obey, pick him up and carry him there. Do not, however, let him come to think that "Bed!" means punishment. Hold a treat over the bed, and as he jumps in to get it, say "Bed". Repeat this many times. Then say "Bed", but don't offer the tidbit. Now, only *after* he jumps in, should you reward him.

The foundations for your Collie's health will be laid in puppyhood by the way he is fed and nurtured.

VIII   Feeding the Adult Collie

As we have seen, the foundations for your Collie's health will be laid in puppyhood by the way he is fed and nurtured. However, it is just as essential that he be properly maintained when he matures. This chapter deals with keeping a Collie of eight months and older in top condition.

The Collie should never be thin. He should always carry plenty of flesh, without being fat and flabby, and he should never appear bony but muscular and hard without being skinny. Rarely will a Collie overeat. Never, in all the years that I have loved and worked with Collies, have I found one who could be called a "pig". So the best thing to do to keep your dog in tip-top condition is to give him all he will eat. He is not going to burst, I promise you. He will have a great deal of maturing to do in his early years, and he will need plenty of really good food to enable him to achieve his final beauty and finish his stature.

It is up to you to provide the correct nourishment. Just as the human being demands a balanced diet, so does the dog, but the nutritional requirements are quite different.

A look at the dog's mouth will show you the job his jaws were made to do. His long canine teeth were fundamentally for tearing away large pieces of flesh, and his very large double teeth at the back were built for cutting rather than for grinding, as ours are.

Ask yourself then, whether an animal with a mouth and teeth like these could ever be statisfied on a diet of slops or minced food. The answer is a big "No"! It is far more natural for your Collie to devour his meat in a gulp than to have it cut up small or minced.

What makes up our dog? About two-thirds of the total weight of an adult dog in good condition consists of water, and of the remaining third, nine-tenths is protein.

On what then should we feed our dog?

Foods for the dog fall into five general classes – meat, milk and cheese, fats, cereals, and vegetables.

Milk and Cheese: *Fresh cows' milk is approximately 90 % water. The water content of cheese varies according to its type, cream cheese being fairly high, and the other types relatively low. Much of the protein and fat from milk is found in cheese.*

Fats: *Fats can be either animal fat found in fresh fatty meat, butter, lard or drippings, vegetable oils and margarine. There may be a small amount of protein in meat fat but this can be discounted.*

Cereals: *Carbohydrates are found mainly in the cereals – wheat, barley, corn, rice, oats; the main intake of cereals for a dog is from biscuits, kibble, and dog meal. Cereals are fairly low in protein (usually only about 10 %) for about 60 % is carbohydrate.*

Vegetables: *Fresh vegetables, whether green or of the root type, are composed of about 80 % water. Dried vegetables – lentils, peas, beans, and so forth – contain very little water, are about 50 % carbohydrate, and are considerably richer in protein than the cereals.*

There is one other small, but oh so very important nutritional element that we have not yet mentioned – vitamins. Vitamins are present only in minute traces in foods, but they are absolutely essential to life.

Vitamins can be divided into two main groups – water-soluble and fat-soluble vitamins. Into the fat-soluble group fall Vitamins A, D, E, and K, and into the water-soluble group, Vitamin C and all the Vitamin B group. Today, almost all the vitamins can be produced chemically in the laboratory, and it should be stressed that they are identical with those found in foods, and that their action on the body is the same. However, it is much more expensive to feed some of the arificially produced vitamins, although they are of tremendous help in time of illness or cases of malnutrition. A word of warning however, if you are feeding chemically produced vitamins of the fat-soluble group, it is essential that you pay careful attention to the quantity for an overdose can lead to serious illness. Table II on page 107 shows the infinitesimal amounts of vitamins required to sustain condition in a Collie.

Commercial Foods

Today, there are so many different kinds of prepared dog food on the market that we must now consider what part these can play in feeding.

The gamin look of the Collie which endears him to everyone.

AKE WINTZELL

The main types are, of course, biscuits, kibble, and meal, canned meat alone, canned meat and cereal, dried meat and fish, and frozen meat. The meal types and some of the biscuits and kibbles and certain canned foods are considered "complete". The others require supplementing, or may be fed as supplements themselves. Undoubtedly, one great advantage is convenience; certainly, when on holiday with the family dog there is nothing that is as easy to use and as reliable. For all prepared foods of the canned or biscuit kind are extremely hygienic; however, during the processing of these foods some nutrients may be destroyed.

The question of cost is one which must be considered, and this depends partly on where one lives. In some parts of the world fresh meat, even in the form of tripe or fish, is much more expensive than in others, and cost will be a deciding question. However, it is not enough to make a straight comparison of the cost of canned meat per pound with the cost of fresh meat because canned and dried meats have certain dietary inadequacies, and the cost of supplementing them must be taken into consideration. Sterilization when canning foods is essential, and this causes partial destruction of certain members of the Vitamin B family, particularly thiamine. As the presence of thiamine stimulates the appetite, one quickly sees how a lack of it could be detrimental to the dog. Sterilization can also cause a slight change in the quality of protein. However, manufacturers now fortify proteins with synthetic additives, but since this is not too easy to do, it is not really the whole answer. It follows then that the most satisfactory means of feeding your adult Collie is on complete commercial foods alone, or on commercial foods plus fresh meat or flesh of some kind.

Your adult Collie should receive two meals a day; if you feed a mixed diet, a breakfast of milk and cereal is good – the cereal can be dog kibble or one of the usual human breakfast cereals. An eight-ounce cup of cereal plus a half to one pint of milk should be enough. To this add, particularly in winter, a little cod liver oil to supply the necessary Vitamins A and D.

His main meal, best given in the evening, can consist of at least one pound of raw meat or the canned equivalent (many adult Collies will eat as much as a pound and a half). This may be given with kibble or biscuit added, whichever your dog prefers. From time to time this main meal can be varied. Give fish instead of meat, and it too can be raw or cooked. Rabbit, poultry, heart, liver, kidneys

This is a blue-eyed merle Collie bred in Sweden. It is a beautiful color, but unfortunately somewhat rare.

and tripe can all take their turn in the dog's diet. Pork, however, should not be fed unless it is very well cooked.

A Collie should have *at least* two or three ounces of fat daily, and this can be added to his food in the form of drippings, pure animal fat, butter, lard, or, failing these, margarine. You may find that your dog will take a while to become accustomed to a new type of diet; he may even refuse to eat for a day or two. Do not be alarmed – a short fast does an adult dog no harm so long as he always has fresh water before him. After refusing to eat for a day he will probably eat avidly whatever is put before him.

Dry Dog Foods

In America, many Collie breeders have found that the simplest, least expensive and most efficient way of feeding is to use one of the demonstrated complete dry diets to which they add about 15 % of fat. The adult dog consumes about one pound of dry food and at least two ounces of fat. As I write this, the cost of dry food is about about 12 cents per pound and fat from the butcher's fat barrel, passed through the meat grinder costs 5 cents per pound, making the dog's ration cost about 13 cents and supplying every known dietary essential.

The cost of vitamins and minerals to the big manufacturers is so little that insuring a complete food can be taken for granted. The big manufacturers maintain their own research kennels and vie with each other in turning out foods of excellent quality. Government regulations prohibit misleading claims on the containers. When the container claims the food is complete, it probably is but for safety's sake, adding fat is inexpensive and it helps to keep the dog plump and the coat in glowing health.

Feeding the Stud Dog

Unless the average, healthy male dog is being used frequently at stud, the above diets should be sufficient. The extra energy needed to produce the seminal fluid discharged in mating is so slight that it need not be considered here.

Feeding the Bitch in Whelp

If your bitch has been carefully reared and maintained until she is ready to mate, little change need be made in her diet until three or four weeks after the mating, but from the fourth to certainly the eighth week she will demand increasingly more food. This should be given to her in high protein form. If you do not use a commercial food her diet should gradually be stepped up, by the sixth week, to at least a pound of meat in mid-morning; the same in the afternoon, and another meal at bed time, probably cereal, kibble with stock, milk, perhaps a boiled egg, or whatever she likes most.

In the very early days of pregnancy a bitch's appetite may fluctuate. Do not let it worry you if she refuses her food for one day, but if she refuses for a longer period, get veterinary advice. Additional calcium should also be given to the bitch in whelp. Remember that you are not feeding her just for herself and her as yet unborn litter, but for those weeks when she alone will be completely responsible for the nourishment of her puppies. To be on the safe side, the addition of raw liver to her diet is extremely important. She need not have very much – four ounces once a week is sufficient – but liver is such a rich source of Vitamin A that its addition in pregnancy is essential. Lack of Vitamin A may cause the death of, or various malformations of the foetus, and for this reason the need for Vitamin A cannot be stressed too much. Liver is also a rich source of thiamine, another essential during pregnancy.

Feeding the Nursing Bitch

In our chapter on breeding we deal with the treatment of the bitch immediately after the whelping. Provided she shows no ill effects, 48 hours after the last puppy is born begin to step up her diet to the peak of her pregnancy period. One cannot be completely dogmatic about the quantity to be given during lactation, because this will vary according to the number of puppies. A bitch with four puppies will obviously not need as much food as one with eight or nine. This additional food should be high in protein content, and the bitch should continue her supplement of cod liver oil and calcium. Nor can I stress too often the absolute necessity of always having water present, for nothing will cause the milk supply to dry up more quickly than the lack of fresh water.

Bitchs' milk is so high in fat content that the addition of 20 % fat to her diet will spare her from using the stored fat on her body.

Nutrient Requirements

A great deal of work on dog nutrition is being done by governmental agencies. This work is not only investigatory but is also necessary because the government sets standards for pet food manufacturers. A summary of some of the findings of the Subcommittee on Canine Nutrition of the National Academy of Sciences condensed into chart form are given here.

Table I will be of interest to those who would like to prepare their own mix, and for those who are curious as to just what goes into a commercial dog food. It is a breakdown of two different meal-type rations.

Table I

Meal-Type Rations for Dogs [1]
(Dry matter 91 %)

	Ration	
Ingredient	1	2
	%	%
Meat and bone meal, 55 % protein	8.00	15.00
Fish meal, 60 % protein	5.00	3.00
Soybean oil meal	12.00	–
Soybean grits	–	19.00
Wheat germ oil meal	8.00	5.00
Skim milk, dried	4.00	2.50
Cereal grains	51.23	–
Corn flakes	–	26.75
Wheat bran	4.00	–
Wheat flakes	–	26.75
Fat, edible	2.00	–
Bone meal, steamed	2.00	–
Brewers yeast, dried	2.00	0.50
Fermentation solubles, dried	1.00	–
Salt, iodized	0.50	0.25
Vitamin A & D feeding oil (2,250 IU of A, 400 IU of D per gm)	0.25	0.50
Riboflavin supplement [2]	–	0.80
Iron oxide	0.02	–

[1] While these rations have been used satisfactorily with some dogs, there is no assurance that all dogs will accept them readily.

[2] BY-500.

Table II lists a dog's requirements in terms of food components per pound of body weight. It is interesting to note that growing puppies (last column) require two or more times as much of each of these nutrients as do adult dogs.

Table II

Nutrient Requirements of Dogs [1]
(Amounts per pound of body weight per day)

	Weight of dog in pounds	Adult maintenance	Growing puppies
Energy (kcal) [2]	5	50	100
	10	42	84
	15	35	70
	30	32	64
	50 and over	31	62
Protein-minimum (gm)		2.0	4.0
Carbohydrate-maximum (gm) [3]		4.6	7.2
Fat (gm)		0.6	1.2
Minerals:			
Calcium (mg)		120	240
Phosphorus (mg)		100	200
Iron (mg)		0.600	0.600
Copper (mg)		0.075	0.075
Cobalt (mg)		0.025	0.025
Sodium Chloride (mg)		170	240
Potassium (mg)		100	200
Magnesium (mg)		5	10
Manganese (mg)		0.050	0.100
Zinc (mg)		0.050	0.100
Iodine (mg)		0.015	0.030
Vitamins:			
Vitamin A (IU) [3]		45	90
Vitamin D (IU) [3]		3	9
Vitamin E (mg)		–	1
Vitamin B_{12} (mg)		0.0003	0.0006
Folic acid (mg)		0.002	0.004
Riboflavin (mg)		0.020	0.040
Pyridoxine (mg)		0.010	0.020
Pantothenic acid (mg)		0.023	0.045
Niacin (mg)		0.110	0.180
Choline (mg)		15	30

While the amount of food required by a dog varies, depending on such things as the dog's own metabolism, activity, environment, and so on, as we have previously noted, the greatest difference will be found between the requirements of a growing dog and an adult.

Table III gives the estimated daily food intake required by dogs of various sizes, broken down into *Requirements for maintenance* – this covers the average non-working dog under normal conditions – and *Requirements for Growth* – these are the amounts of food required by a growing dog. While some adjustments in these amounts may be required for your own pet, they do serve as guidelines when estimating how much to feed your dog. An old dog will probably require less food than indicated here, while a pregnant or nursing bitch will require more.

Table II footnotes

[1] Symbols-gm = gram; mg = milligram; IU = International Unit.

[2] Values listed are for gross or calculated energy. Biologically available energy is ordinarily 75-85 per cent of the calculated.

[1] The values shown are based upon dry and canned foods containing 91 and 28 per cent dry matter. Moisture has been included to indicate general level of composition rather than as a requirement. There is no evidence that carbohydrate as such is required, but since it occurs as a part of many dog-food ingredients, a maximum value has been suggested.

[2] The 0.6 and 018 mg quantity of crystalline vitamin A is equal to 2000 and 600 IU, respectively. One mg vitamin A alcohol = 3,333 IU of vitamin A. One mg beta carotene = 1,667 IU of vitamin-A activity. For dogs carotene is approximately one-half as valuable as vitamin-A alcohol.

[3] These amounts of pure vitamin D correspond to 120 and 40 IU per pound of feed.

[4] As alpha tocopherol.

Table III

Estimated daily food Intakes required by dogs of various sizes

| | Requirements for Maintenance | | | |
| | Dry type foods [1] | | Canned dog food [2] | |
Weight of dog	Per lb body wt	Per dog	Per lb body wt	Per dog
lbs	lbs	lbs	lbs	lbs
5	0.040	0.20	0.120	0.60
10	0.033	0.33	0.101	1.01
15	0.028	0.42	0.085	1.27
20	0.027	0.54	0.081	1.60
30	0.025	0.75	0.077	2.30
50	0.025	1.25	0.075	3.74
70	0.025	1.75	0.075	5.23
110	0.024	2.64	0.074	8.22

| | Requirements for Growth | | | |
| | Dry type foods [1] | | Canned dog food [2] | |
Weight of dog	Per lb body wt	Per dog	Per lb body wt	Per dog
lbs	lbs	lbs	lbs	lbs
5	0.080	0.40	0.240	1.20
10	0.066	0.66	0.202	2.02
15	0.056	0.84	0.190	2.54
20	0.054	1.08	0.160	3.20
30	0.050	1.50	0.154	4.60
50	0.050	2.60	0.150	7.48
70	0.050	3.50	0.150	10.46
110	0.048	5.28	–	–

Dry foods contain 6-12 per cent moisture. Calculations of the amounts of dry food required have been based on energy supplied by food containing 91 per cent dry matter, 76 per cent protein plus carbohydrate, 5 per cent fat and 10 per cent ash, fiber and other inert material. This supplies a calculated 1583 kcal per pound, of which it is estimated that 80 per cent or 1266 kcal are digestible.

[2] Calculated on the basis of 28 per cent dry matter and the same nutrient ratios as in 1, with the total and available energy calculated as 490 and 415 (85 per cent of the total) kcal per pound.

A Collie's head must blend with his mane and ruff, and yet be set off harmoniously.

A Collie will frequently train himself to do many things on his own. Here is one example. Climbing trees is not included in the list of tricks to be taught a Collie, yet in order to be near his beloved mistress this Collie taught himself.

IX Training Your Collie

During those first days after you had brought your puppy home and were housebreaking him, he was completely receptive and obedient because he was then wholly dependent on you. But as a puppy grows, so does a spirit of independence. He will want to spread his wings, and he will be irked by constantly being made to obey. Collies, probably more than most breeds, go through this recalcitrant period. It is a time that I call their "close-eared" period, because they just don't want to listen. This usually occurs when they are from four to five months old, and it may, unfortunately, last as long as four months.

A Collie is very sensitive to criticism. It is seldom necessary to physically punish him although at times a good scolding may be in order.

If, during this time, you persist in nagging your puppy and making him obey, you will end up with a dog whose will is broken. It is better to forestall him. By "forestalling" I mean that you should be able to anticipate an act of disobedience. For instance, you want to go for a walk. You want to put his leash on. But you wait until you are outdoors to do so. You call him and he refuses to come. If you had put that leash on in the house, he would not have had a chance to disobey, and you would not have had to discipline him for disobedience,

In like manner, his bad chewing habits may reappear. This is often the case because as he starts to teethe he wants something on which to cut his new teeth. If he possibly can, he will ignore your telling him to stop chewing. So it is up to you to see that there is nothing for him to chew on when you leave him alone in the house. Give him his toys in the room where you shut him – the bathroom, for instance. So, try to forestall any bad behavior rather than wait until it has been committed and chastisement becomes necessary. This will be pleasanter for the puppy and for you.

Because of the Collie's tremendously long association with man and his innate desire to always please, he is much more sensitive to correction. Therefore, a little latitude at this time, without losing control of your dog, or letting him get away with murder, will eventually repay you 100 %, because you will end up with a trusting, happy, willing-to-please, obedient and faithful companion.

The training and housebreaking of the young puppy is dealt with in an earlier chapter. Let us now consider what to do as our Collie begins to grow up. The Collie is extremely responsive to training because, as I have said already, his great desire is to please. The first step in training any animal is to establish a rapport between you. This is easy with the Collie.

One of the first essentials in training is to establish control, not only your control of your dog, but also control of yourself. You cannot hope to train a dog if you yourself are inclined to lose your temper. This you must never do. If you do, the dog will lose his respect for you; furthermore, you will hurt his feelings because a Collie is such a sensitive creature.

Never begin a training session with one eye on the clock. Always choose a period when you will not be rushed. If things don't go well, you will always have that extra bit of time to achieve what you set out to do, for the one thing that is fatal is to stop a training period when the dog has the upper hand.

It is absolute that the Collie be always trained by kindness and praise, and by the giving of tidbits along with the praise. He may, of course, receive verbal correction, but never physical punishment. The mere fact that you are displeased with him will, for a dog of his temperament, be correction enough. Since a dog cannot understand our vocabulary, in training him it is important to keep the words of command to a minimum, and to keep them always the same. You cannot possibly expect him to obey if you tell him "here" today and "come" tomorrow. To him, those two words have entirely different meanings because of their sounds.

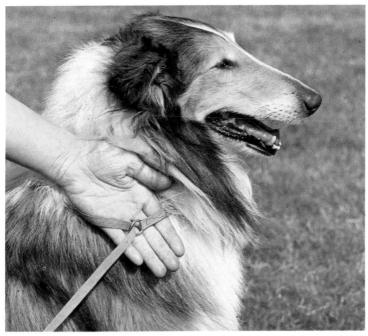

A leather or nylon slip or choke collar is preferable for the Collie.

Equipment

Very little is required in the way of equipment for early training – a plain flat collar, a slip or choke collar and leads of various lengths. A six foot training lead and a twenty foot check rope are essential. Three-foot and twelve-foot leads, while helpful, may or may not be used.

Slip Collar

The first thing to teach your dog is to walk properly on a collar and lead, and for this a leather slip or choke collar is, in my opinion, best. Nylon may be substituted for leather. I believe a Collie's hearing is so sensitive that he finds the noise of the chain on his neck distasteful. I have always found that a plain leather slip collar is perfectly adequate and very useful.

Heeling

In the chapter on early training you were told how to teach your puppy to walk around with a collar and lead, but now you must teach him to do more than just follow you; he must walk beside you properly. For this, put him on your left side, taking the handle of the leash in your right hand, and as you step forward starting with your left foot, call him by name, adding the command "Heel". At the same time, give the slack of the lead a sharp little jerk with your left hand to alert him. If, as I expect, he has immediately stepped off with you, now is the moment for praise. This is why the leash is held in the right hand – to leave your other hand free to correct or pat him as the case may be.

To teach your dog to "Heel", put him on your left side, taking the handle of the leash in your right hand, and as you step forward starting with your left foot, call him by name, adding the command "Heel!".

SALLY ANNE THOMPSON

To teach your dog to "Sit", press down on his rump with one hand while pulling up and back at his lead with the other.

Sit

Keep walking forward, praising and talking to him as you go, and then stop suddenly. At this moment, again with your left hand, press down on his rump, simultaneously raising his head by means of the leash in your right hand and give the command, "Sit". These together should bring him into a sitting position. It should not be long before he gets the idea so well that he will automatically come into a sitting position as you stop, simply on the word "Sit".

Turns

As he becomes gradually more expert at heeling, make sharp turns as you walk, each time giving a little jerk on the lead to keep his attention on you, and at the same time add the command, "Heel". Do not forget to praise, praise, praise. As he becomes more and more expert, he will perform this very useful exercise as well off the lead as on. Please, never take him out on a road without a lead. Even the best trained dog can have an accident. A car may backfire and frighten him off the sidewalk, and within a moment you might have a dead dog. It is just not worth the risk.

Come

Your next task is to teach the meaning of the word "Come". Up until now he has probably come when called, if it suited him and very often it did, but now you want a really reliable dog who will come every time you call him. Take him out on his collar and a long lead, or a light cord, and make him sit or lie down. Walk a little away from him, keeping the end of the lead in your hand and, when you are ready, give the command, "Come". At the same time jerk the lead, pulling and calling the dog towards you. If you wish, you

SALLY ANNE THOMPSON

When your dog is being walked at "Heel," he should "Sit" automatically each time you stop.

can also run backwards a few steps to set the exercise more definitely in your dog's mind. Soon you will be able to leave him and, without holding the leash, be able to walk away and have him come when you call.

Sometimes he will be much more anxious to follow his own desires as for instance, to explore that lovely smell or to discover to where that bird flew off. If your dog is guilty of this, take him out on his walk as usual, take his lead off to let him run, but have, unknown to him, a long, fine cord attached to his collar. If he does not come at once when you call, jerk the cord, and that one sharp, unexpected jerk, firmly applied, may well cure him for the rest of his life. This "secret" cord can be a very strong fishing line, so light that the dog will not know it is there.

The two training exercises to be given next may at some time save your pet's life, for they have often saved lives in the past. These are the exercises "Down" and "Stay".

Down

To teach your dog "Down", put him on the collar and lead. Have him sit on your left, then pass the lead under the raised instep of your right shoe, the slack, as always, coiled in your right hand. Then on the command "Down", press down on his shoulders with your left hand; at the same time pulling him down by pulling *up* on

This is a young dog and his glorious Collie coat has not yet fully appeared. It may take two or three years to mature. The round object at which he is staring so intently is a ball which he is learning to catch.

LOUISE VAN DER MEID

While it may not be necessary to reward your dog each time he performs well, a tidbit given from time to time will encourage him.

the lead. Repeat this exercise as often as necessary, and give him plenty of praise each time you get his chin onto the ground. You will soon find that you have a dog that will drop as you give the command. Next, put him a little distance from you, and give the command again. He will gradually learn to "Down" even at a great distance. Now do you begin to see the tremendous value of this command? Imagine yourself with your dog headed straight toward you. You see danger approaching on a line between you. That one command "Down", reacted to instantly, may well save your dog's life.

Stay

To teach this, put him into either the "Sit" or "Down" position,

SALLY ANNE THOMPSON

"Shake hands" is an appealing trick and one easily taught. Press against your Collie's right shoulder with your left hand, and as he lifts his paw take it and repeat the command "Shake hands!"

whichever you wish, with his lead on. Give the command, "Stay", and back a few paces away, keeping an eye on him all the time. Should he rise, give him a further command of "Sit" or "Down", and then add the word "Stay". This I find a difficult exercise to teach a Collie, because of his desire to be with his master. So, great patience will probably be required. There is nothing for you to do but go back each time, make him "Sit" or "Down" again, and repeat the command "Stay" until gradually you arrive at a time when you can leave him for an hour, if necessary, without his coming to look for you, knowing full well that you will find him where you left him on your return.

There are a number of other exercises demanded in the Obedience Training ring, but these are covered far more expertly and more fully than space permits here in books devoted to that subject. A

particularly good one is "Pet Library's Dog Training Guide" by
Jack Kenworthy, in this series.

Social Behavior

Recent genetic studies emphasize the importance of heredity in the
development of dog behavior. Heredity has an important effect on
almost every trait tested. One study was by Drs. J. P. Scott and
John L. Fuller working at the Jackson Laboratory, Bar Harbor,
Maine. They worked with five breeds of dogs representing the major
groups – Wire-Hair Fox Terrier, American Cocker Spaniel, Afri-
can Basenji, Shetland Sheepdog and the Beagle.

Among other things, they found that sex does have definite effects upon the aggresive tendencies of dogs and upon the dominance
order, but not upon their trainability nor their ability to solve problems. This means then that the male is more dominant (the pack
leader) and aggressive, but that the female is his equal when it comes
to training and intelligence.

Inherited emotional traits profoundly influence performance. Although the various breeds differed widely in emotional and moti-
vational characteristics, no one breed was superior to any other in
solving problems. Detailed statistical analysis indicates that there
is a highly complex relationship between the basic genetic inheritance and its final effect upon behavior.

Perhaps the most important of their findings, so far as the pet
owner is concerned, is that there is a critical period in the puppy's
life which exerts a lasting influence upon its adult behavior and
ability to adjust to human relationships. A puppy removed from its
mother and littermates at the age of six to eight weeks, and brought
into a home and family environment, where it is handled and petted,
has a far better chance of becoming a well-adjusted dog in its relationships with both people and other dogs than the one left behind
in the kennel where, although it is adequately fed and housed, it is
not given the advantage of human handling. For a puppy to turn
out well then, it should be brought into the home as early as possible
(before it is eight weeks old and certainly not after 13 weeks) if
it has never known the human touch. Let me emphasize that this contact with humans need not necessarily be extensive. Even picking
a dog up gently once a day is sufficient to establish the proper
rapport.

A Collie should *never* be bathed routinely. The only time a Collie should be bathed is when he's gotten into something he shouldn't and there's no other way to clean him.

X   Grooming Your Collie

Unlike many breeds, Collies do not need a great deal of trimming. Therefore, the grooming tools needed are neither numerous nor complicated. The ones you will need to do the job thoroughly – and by that I mean to groom a Collie for the show ring – are:

Radial nylon brush

Wide-toothed comb, preferably steel

Fine-toothed comb, steel

Sharp scissors, straight ones

Curved scissors

Spray bottle

Warm water

Soap

Sponge

Towel

Nailclippers

Large quantity of precipitated chalk. If you cannot get precipitated chalk, French chalk will do, or even cornflour.

There are two schools of thought on the subject of Collie grooming. Some owners belong to the "don't groom" school, others to the "groom daily". I advise you, if your Collie is a house pet, to place yourself somewhere between these two extremes. In my opinion, more harm than good is done by grooming a Collie daily; but to leave him totally ungroomed is to ask for equal trouble, because his coat will mat. Then, when you want to get him into good condition, it will be extremely difficult.

Brushing your Collie really hard once a week is about all the grooming he should need. He should never, and I repeat *never*, be bathed routinely. The only time a Collie should be bathed is when he's gotten into something he shouldn't and there's no other way to clean him. If you want his white parts to look sparkingly clean.

The hair behind a Collie's ears is particularly soft and silky, and this is the hair most likely to mat; so check this area often and comb it when necessary.

SALLY ANNE THOMPSON

then, of course, wash them with a little warm water and detergent. But to bathe a Collie all over is to destroy completely the natural oils in his coat, and it will take many weeks before they all build up again. Mud usually presents no problem because most of it dries up and falls out of the coat and a final brushing will get rid of what little remains. If you want your dog to look especially clean on some occasion, chalk through his white parts, then brush the chalk well out, as described in the section on Show Ring Grooming.

Go Easy on the Combing

The hair behind a Collie's ears is particularly soft and silky, and this is the hair most likely to mat; so check this area often. This, I think, is the only part of the coat that should be combed. To comb the coat all over is only to break and destroy it, but you will need a fine comb to remove the mats from behind the ears. If such mats form, they can interfere with the correct ear carriage. Very often, the erect ear of a Collie is traceable to the fact that there are mats and hairballs behind it; so pay great attention to this point, even if your dog is only a house pet, not a show ring prospect.

Shedding

There is, however, one exception to the "no comb" rule. When your dog begins to cast his coat in real earnest for the seasonal shedding, put your comb to work. Comb it at least daily, twice daily if you have the time, until the day arrives when no more hair will come out, and the Collie looks nearly naked. For the sooner you get rid of the dead hair, the faster the new coat will come in, and you will, once more, be able to take pride in your lovely Collie.

Ear Care

Daily ear examination is always wise. Never wash out a dog's ears with soap and water – not even the outer ear. If water gets deep into the ear, it is almost impossible to get it out, and it can present all kinds of problems. The best way to clean ears is with a cotton swab dipped in peroxide, alcohol or olive oil. Never probe deeper into the ear than you can see. If the ears seem unusually sensitive, or have a foul smell, it is wise to consult your vet. There are several good medicated dog earswashes on the market. Ask your favorite pet shop owner to recommend one.

Ear Mange (Otodectic), sometimes called canker, is caused by rather large mites which infect the ear canal, causing painful irritation. The dog repeatedly shakes his head and scratches, crying and whining meanwhile. Soak a layer of cotton in mineral oil, wrap it around your index finger, and clean the ear with this gently.

Otodectes cynotis. This is the ear mite that causes ear canker in dogs.

There are many excellent cures for ear canker but scrupulous cleanliness helps most of all. The dark red discharge has a heavy unpleasant smell which will warn you of the mite's presence if the dog's misery and scratching at the base of the ear has not already pointed it out. Quite often a dog has been deemed "crabby" or shy when all that ailed him was ear mange.

Eye Care

The eyes frequently collect foreign matter like seeds and pollen when the dog roams through high grass or ground cover. These can be irritating and, after such a venture, the eyes should be washed out with a commercial dog eye wash, or if none is at hand, luke-warm water. Some owners recommend a mild boric acid solution (2 %) but this writer does not use it – too many dogs have had their eyes injured by boric acid.

Eyes that are constantly mattered-up and watering are suspect, and a veterinarian should be consulted. It may be the result of entropion – a hereditary condition in which the eyelids turn inward, or ectropion, when they turn outward. However, simple conjunctivitis – inflamed and watering eyes – can usually be dealt with at home. There are several reliable preparations on the market to combat it. Sometimes the gentle rubbing of sterile codliver oil on the upper and lower eyelid helps.

Any mucus in the eye-corners can be removed with a cotton-tipped swab dipped in lukewarm water.

Show Ring Grooming

Grooming for the show ring is a different matter. Again it is not necessary to groom him every day, even if he is a show dog, and certainly not to comb him; but when you decide to take your dog to a show, begin some weeks in advance to prepare him for the great day. This preparation need only consist of a regular, let us say, twice weekly grooming, and at this stage, I would suggest, also, that you begin to do any necessary trimming, because if you mistakenly over-trim two weeks before the show, you will at least have a chance for nature to correct your errors. It is for this reason that I start with a discussion of trimming rather than grooming.

The legs are the only parts of the Collie that need careful trimming, and it depends on where you live and where you show, which legs you trim. In Britain, only the hind legs are trimmed; in America both the front and the hind legs come in for a certain amount of trimming.

Let us start with the hind legs, since their trimming is common to both countries. They need more trimming too. From the hocks downwards, the hind legs will probably carry a great deal of long hair which must be trimmed off. Use a pair of straight scissors, trimming from the hock downwards. First of all, brush or comb the hair out, so that it stands at right-angles to the leg, and then holding your scissors points down and parallel to the skin, cut in a downward direction. You will probably find it advisable to take the hair off in three of four scissorings rather than doing it all at once. It is almost as if you were mowing a lawn, except that you always go back to the same end to start.

The art is to round the hair off at the sides without leaving a sort of ditch in the middle with longer hair standing up on each side. Shorten the side hairs until they blend in with the hairs on the front of the legs.

In America, it is the custom to cut some hair off the front legs as well.

Examine your dog's front legs until you find the black pad, which is just about under the knee. From this pad downwards the long hair should be treated exactly the same as the hair on the back legs – tidied off and feathered in well with the short hairs on the front.

Your next job is to tidy up your dog's feet. Take small scissors, preferably curved, and cut the hair between the pads away under each foot. Do not cut between the toes. Now trim right round the outside of the paw until the hair is short, outlining the foot correctly. Then trim the hair round the toenails. This is probably easier to do with straight scissors. Have the dog stand on the foot you are trimming, preferably on a perfectly flat hard surface like concrete. Watch that you have not left any odd strands of hair, and if so, clip them off before starting on the next foot. When you have done this successfully four times, you will be well on your way.

Some owners trim off the long whiskers on the dog's head, on either side of the muzzle and off the cheeks and eyebrows. This is something I never do. I consider it cruel. The fact that one can rarely

Trimming the long whiskers on the dog's head is not recommended by the author. It is customary, however, in some countries to trim them before the dog is shown. To be safe, hold your fingers over his eyes and use curved, blunt scissors.

LOUISE VAN DER MEID

cut these without an assistant to hold the dog proves that a dog's whiskers are just as sensitive as those of a cat, and no one would ever think of cutting them off a cat. However, as it is customary in some countries to trim these whiskers before the dog is shown, I can only add that if it must be done, do it with the curved scissors. To be safe, hold your fingers over his eyes so that if he moves suddenly you won't stab them. Whisker trimming should be done only at the last moment – the night before the show at the earliest – because whiskers grow back quite rapidly, and you would not want your Collie to appear in the ring with a "five o'clock shadow".

Returning now to the trimming that can be started a couple of weeks before the show, look at your dog's ears and see whether around them, either in front or back, there are long straggly strands of hair. If so, they should be carefully removed. Do this with the thumb and finger, twisting them out a few at a time. It causes only a twinge of pain – like plucking eyebrows and if you have two weeks in which to complete the job, a few hairs can be stripped out each day without creating a hardship for either of you. Do not remove too many hairs, as that would tend to give him a hard expression. Where the hairs are long and straggly, or curling inside the ear, they should certainly be removed.

Having performed this initial trimming, keep an eye on the ears so that, if the hairs grow back before the show, you have time to pluck them. The speed at which each hair grows, particularly on the hind legs, varies tremendously from dog to dog. Some Collies rarely need this part of the leg trimmed at all. Others look like Clydesdale horses, and seem to grow their feathering in a matter of days.

Now take a brush. For this job I prefer a radial nylon brush. It gets down to the skin of the dog, and the spaces between the bristles allow greater penetration. With this brush go over the dog from head to foot, starting at his head end and working down, making absolutely sure that no mats are left anywhere. If you do find a mat, get to work with your wide-toothed comb until each hair is separated again. After this initial preparation, done some two weeks before the show, go over him at least every second day with your nylon brush, just to make sure that no fresh mats are forming, taking special pains behind the ears. Be sure that the soft hair there does not bunch up and become unsightly.

This brings us up to the day before the show. Now, you will again do everything I have suggested, and one or two other things as well.

A radial nylon brush gets down to the skin of the dog, and the spaces between the bristles allow for greater penetration. With this brush go over the dog from head to foot.

Check your dog's toenails, making sure they are not too long. This, in fact, in Collies is rare, but if you think that the white of the toenail is too far extended from the quick (which can be seen showing pink within the white) snip the tip of the nail. Tidy up the feet again if necessary.

It is rarely necessary to clip a Collie's toenails. If you think that the white of the nail is too far extended from the quick (which can be seen showing pink within the white), snip the tip of the nail.

Next, you will want a bucket of warm water with a detergent. Put the dog's legs one by one into this bucket, washing them throroughly until they are sparkling clean. Also, wash his white shirt front, and his collar and tail tip if it is white. Rub the dog until he is nearly dry, then chalk these white parts. Brush the chalk well into the foot, the leg, the collar and the tail tip. Leave the chalk in the fur at least overnight. If you think there is a chance of his getting dirty on the way to the show, or at the entrance to the show, leave the chalk in until after your arrival because, when you brush it out, any dirt acquired on the journey will come with it. However, by the time you get to the show there probably won't be a great deal of chalk left, because the dog will have shaken it out during the night.

Remember to arrive at the show in plenty of time. You will probably need at least an hour to get yourself and your dog in readiness. The white parts must almost certainly be rechalked on arrival, and it is often wise to wash and chalk the legs once more. You cannot, of course, wash shirt front and collar again at this late stage because they would take too long to dry. After rechalking your dog, go over him again with your nylon brush, until each hair is standing out separately. You can also run your comb through the hair as well, if you think that this will help. Remember, though, that you must never take your dog into the show ring with chalk still on him. Brush out every particle before going into the ring. If the judge detects chalk in the dog's coat, he may well disqualify him. So be careful.

Now for one of the final touches: Take a spray – an ordinary spray bottle – filled with either fresh water, or 50 % water and 50 % of one of the many advertised coat dressings, and parting the hair at appropriate places spray it against his skin. Your object is to make the undercoat really damp, but not the long hairs on top. A damp undercoat will help to keep the top coat standing off, giving the impression that your dog has a larger coat than he really has. This spraying should be done straight along his back and on his sides, and on his flanks. The start to brush, and brush, and brush, and brush, and brush. The object is to get him nearly dry, but not quite dry, and leave the top coat standing off.

This last should be done just before he goes into the ring. Then, as a last minute touch, make certain that his plus-fours are beautifully brushed out, that the hair under his tail is equally well-treated, and that the feathers on his front legs stand out as they should. Then take your nylon brush and, very gently, flatten the long top coat the

In preparation for a show, wash his white apron front, each leg, and the collar and tail tips if they are white. Rub the dog until he is nearly dry, then chalk these white parts.

SALLY ANNE THOMPSON

full length of his back bone from head to tail root and just a little over his sides as well, because you do not want him to go into the ring looking like a large woolly bear. His coat must appear to fit him, but it must also appear to be beautiful and heavy.

If your dog is to be shown at a number of shows within a short period, all that you will need to do, having got him ready for his first show, is to check regularly that he is not becoming matted behind the ears, that his feet remain tidy, and that the feathering on his back legs does not need cutting. Other than this, the pre-show day damping and chalking and regular brushing are all that should be necessary after your arrival at the show.

Learning to care for a dog is a fine lesson in responsibility. It has been observed that boys who have dogs seldom become juvenile delinquents.

This is a scene at an outdoor dog show in England. However, the scene would be the same anywhere in the world where dogs are being shown. The lady in the center is snapping her fingers to attract her dog's attention so that he will look alert.

XI Showing Your Collie

The chief purpose of a dog show is to accord dog owners the opportunity to exhibit their dogs in competition with others of the same breed to win points toward a Championship title, and that accomplished, to win such additional honors as Best of Breed, Best of Group, and – no greater glory than this – Best of Show.

Idealistically, the purpose of a show is to improve the quality of all purebred dogs in general and, in our case, Collies in particular. A show is not just a "beauty contest" as some detractors claim. It is a sporting event, whether you attend as a spectator or as a competitor. So remember this – it is a *sport* – if you do decide to enter your dog in competition, enter with a sportsmanlike attitude. If you can't win without bragging or lose without bitterness (to say nothing of "putting down" your dog), better forget the whole idea here and now.

The ears of a Collie should be set well up on the head and tipped forward. A little help with a moleskin prop, a liquid adhesive, at 5 to 6 months may be necessary to keep them up. During teething the ears may go up or down, but they should never be allowed to stay up for more than a single day. In addition to the moleskin prop, the ears are weighted so that they will tip forward.

LOUISE VAN DER MEID

American Shows

All American dog shows in which Collies can win points toward their championship are held under the auspices and rules of the American Kennel Club (51 Madison Avenue, New York, N.Y. 10003), and it is there you must write for information concerning shows in your area.

The AKC shows fall into one of the two main classes, called Point shows and Match shows. Point shows may be undertaken by a club only after it has satisfactorily conducted a series of Match shows. The latter are more informal and are designed primarily for the pleasure of local club members and exhibitors. Young dogs frequently receive their first show experience at Match shows.

It is the Point Shows which are the more demanding. It is in one of these, and in one of these only, that a Collie can win points toward his American Championship. To earn the title, the "Ch". which is frequently shown as a prefix to a dog's name, the dog must show its superiority over a certain number of other dogs under different judges at a number of shows. Theoretically the title can be gained through wins at three shows. More often it requires thirteen attempts – sometimes thirty; dogs have even been known to make sixty tries before they have earned the title. To become a champion, a dog must win 15 points. These points are awarded on a scale drawn up by the AKC. The country is divided into four groups in which points for each breed are figured on the basis of national registrations and previous show entries for that area. Five points is the highest number that can be won at any one show. A dog must win two shows with three points or more under at least two different judges.

At an American dog show, the entries are judged by breed in five different classes, separated by sex. There is a class for Puppies (the dog must be over 6 months of age but under 12).

American Champion Coronation Blue Angel is being posed by Clint Harris, a professional handler from Louisville, Kentucky. Many show dog owners prefer to have professional handlers train and show their dogs while they sit at ringside and applaud.

LOUISE VAN DER MEID

The Novice class is for dogs over 6 months old that have not won three first prizes in that class nor a first prize in any of the regular classes – Puppy class excepted. Only dogs born in the United States or Canada can compete in this class.

The Bred-by-Exhibitor class is for dogs (except champions) which are owned by the breeder, and must be shown by the breeder or a member of his immediate family.

The American-Bred class is for all dogs except champions. They must have been born in the United States of a mating that also took place in that country.

The Open class is for any dog six months of age or older that has not won its championship. All foreign-bred dogs must enter this class, except that Canadian-bred puppies can enter the Puppy class. The Open class for Collies is divided by color.

The winners of each of these five classes then compete in the Winners' class for a purple ribbon and championship points.

Unless you have had experience in showing dogs, and your Collie shows exceptionally fine promise, it is a good policy to have him make his debut in a sanctioned Match show. At these events tension is less than at a Point show and advice will be given freely by the more experienced Collie fanciers and by the judge himself.

British Shows

In Britain there are four main types of shows. Starting with the lowest, which should really be a training ground for young stock and new exhibitors alike, they have the Sanction show. Such a show, if covering more than one breed, may not comprise more than twenty classes, and if for one breed only, not more than ten. Such a show is open only to club members. This type of show is frequently held in the evening. Such shows can also be a valuable training ground for judges. At a Sanction show no dog who has won a Challenge Certificate, nor more than a certain number of first prizes, is eligible to compete.

Next up the line is the Limited show. Here again only members of the promoting club may compete, and again no winners of Challenge Certificates are eligible, and again the number of classes is controlled usually by the size of the venue.

Then comes the Open show which is open to all, members or not, at which if so desired, Champions may compete, although no points toward a Championship are available. An Open show may not schedule more than fifty classes without special permission if it is an "unbenched" show – that is to say, if there are no benches on which the dogs can be placed. A benched Open show can have an unlimited number of classes, provided the venue is large enough, and approval has been obtained from the Kennel Club.

For all these shows, the selection of the judges is entirely the responsibility of the group sponsoring each particular show, and that group must bear the brunt of any and all complaints. The Kennel Club does not even have to be informed of the choice of judges until the schedule is published. A judge in Britain is not licensed by any governing body as are judges in the USA.

Finally come the Championship shows, and it is at such shows only that a dog may gain awards which count towards the title of Champion. I have already mentioned that in Britain a dog, to become a Champion, must obtain three Challenge Certificates under three different judges. During the year there are 24 sets of CCs on offer for Rough Collies, five of these sets at Specialty Shows, the others at all-breed Championship shows. A "set of CCs" means one for a dog (male) and one for a bitch at each show. The winner of the Best of Breed award does not gain anything further towards the title, simply the one CC. Furthermore, in Britain, dogs which have already obtained the title of Champion complete in the regular Open class, and so, to gain a CC, it is often necessary to beat an established Champion. It is not the same as in America where the win by a Champion of Best of Breed, for instance, does not interfere with the up-and-coming dog taking points toward his Championship title. Thus a British Championship is much more difficult to earn than its counterpart in the USA.

A British show can schedule as many classes for each sex as it pleases. The possibilities are almost limitless, but as a general rule there are about 12 classes for each sex at every Championship show, the classes being divided by age or previous wins. At no show in Britain may a dog under six months old be exhibited, but there is no upper age limit.

Ring Training

If you intend to show your Collie, start with ring training at home. The judge will expect you to parade your dog along with all the

If you intend to show your dog, start with ring training at home. He should learn early to show off to his very utmost, keeping his ears exactly where they should be, his tail down, and looking like a million dollars. This $3\frac{1}{2}$ month old tricolor show prospect is named Lady Muffet of Heather. She is champion-sired and shows great promise.

other entries several times around the ring before he examines each dog separately. Therefore, your Collie must be willing to walk freely and happily on a loose lead. For his preliminary examination the judge sends the exhibitors round in a counter-clockwise direction so that the dog is always nearer to him than the handler. In other words, your dog must walk on your left. Do not keep him on such a loose lead that he can run up close behind the dog in front and sniff at him from behind, and so upset them both, nor should you let him drag back on his lead, making a nuisance of himself to the dog behind. If you have trained him properly to heel on lead, this should present no great problem. Try to find some local ring training class which you can attend. In most countries there are training classes for dogs of almost every breed, and further, many breed clubs, including possibly your local Collie club, will hold ring-craft classes. In this way you can become accustomed to what will happen before you invade the ring yourself.

After the judge has made the dogs do several tours of the ring, he will then call each dog out by itself. He will go over the dog from nose to tail tip assessing as he goes. Therefore, the importance of teaching your dog to stand still under such handling and not becoming frightened or aggressive. The judge will then probably ask you to move your dog apart from the others and this too should be done on a loose lead with the dog moving freely and happily. Next, your dog will be expected to come to attention and show off his ears. For this, he should have been taught to erect them when he is tempted by a tidbit. This will not prove difficult. Let your dog stand beside you while you are cutting up his food. He will probably watch with his ears in an alert position. If you throw him a tiny bit from time to time, he will come to expect it and always keep his ears up when there is food around. If at the same time you snap your fingers or make some other identifying noise, he will come to associate this with holding up his ears.

As I said in an earlier chapter, always get to the show in plenty of time. This is even more true of your first show, for you will want to do the grooming and get your dog ready, and you will want time to accustom him and yourself to your new surroundings. Let him investigate things, go with him, encourage him, talk to him. Do not let him be overwhelmed by the multitude of dogs and the crowds of people, particularly if it is his very first show. However, do not keep trailing him around the show all day. If it is a bench show, of which more later, he will have his own particular corner where he can rest, either with you beside him, or – if he is contented with you out of sight – alone and asleep. Don't expect your dog to show his best if you drag him around, particularly on a hot day, and get him tired and confused before the judging even commences.

At this, his first show and at all subsequent shows, give him plenty of encouragement so that he will know that going to a show means a day spent with you, and that it will be a happy and a cheerful one.

If you own more than one dog, you have only to watch his behavior when he returns home from the show to know whether or not he has enjoyed himself. He goes up to the other dogs, he swanks, he shows off, he tells them what a lovely day he has had all by himself without their hindering him or competing for your attention.

When entering your dog in a show, you will have to take his age into consideration because age governs, in part, the classes for which

Is there any lovelier way to depict summer time? Our model is Such-a-Struggle from Shiel.

SALLY ANNE THOMPSON

he may be eligible. If your Collie is a male and under nine months of age and you have entered him in the Puppy class, then his six-to-nine month old class will be the first in the ring. This will not give you much chance to find out just what is expected of you. So, if Collies are to be the first judged, try to go to a show before the one in which you are entered. Watch the Collie classes so that you may see exactly what occurs.

However, you may find that the time for the judging of Collies is half way through the day, with other breeds being judged before yours. The procedure with all breeds is roughly the same. Get to a ring, watch what goes on, and find out what to do before you take the plunge.

Your dog may be entered in one or more classes, especially if he is still young and eligible. But, it is not usual to enter a dog in more than one class, except in Great Britain, where there is a real clutter of classes for any one breed, and a dog may be entered in as many as six or eight. In America, the dog has just as much chance of winning his championship by winning one class only as he would have if he were entered in two or three; the young dog, entered only in the Puppy Class, has time to go back and rest and to return fresh to the ring when the unbeaten dogs meet each other.

At the end of the judging of any particular sex, all the winners of the various classes are called together into the ring for the judge to choose his final Best of Winners. This is the moment when you want your dog to show off to his very utmost, keeping his ears exactly where they should be, his tail down, and looking like a million dollars. How much cooperation you are going to get from him at this important moment will depend upon how well you have trained him at home. If your dog has been beaten in any of his classes, he is not, of course, eligible to compete in this Winner's Class.

Although the winner's title and the championship points may occasionally go to a puppy, it is more usual for these to be taken by the winner of either the American Bred or the Open classes. So, if your dog is really in form, enter him for one of these, but remember that here he will meet the stiffest competition, the most experienced handlers, and dogs who are nearly if not already champions. But if you think that you or your dog are not yet ready for this red-hot competition, keep him in the lower classes – Puppy, if he is eligible, in the Novice Class if there is one, or maybe in a class for his own coat color. Which you choose is entirely up to you.

If the show is for one breed only, it is known as a "Specialty" show. You will find that there are a greater variety of classes for Collies at Specialties than at shows which are open to all breeds. At these Specialty shows you can have tremendous fun and learn a great deal because there is more time to talk and go about things in a leisurely way.

In any show your dog will have to compete against dogs handled by professional handlers. In the United States the man in this profession is usually so expert that he can get the best out of any dog. If when showing your own dog, a professional handler eyes him and tells you the dog has special merits and that he would like to handle him for you, it may be to your advantage to make such an arrangement.

A professional handler will take your dog to his own establishment, groom him and train him. The man fills his truck or station wagon with many dogs and goes from show to show making "show circuits," as they are called. By taking your dog to so many shows, the handler advertises him and eventually makes him a champion by accumulating 15 points. Once a champion, if it is a male, owners of bitches will want to breed to him and the possession of such a dog can increase one's income, sometimes by several thousand dollars a year. If the animal is a bitch, her puppies will be in greater demand and worth more money.

Professional handlers charge a fixed amount for handling at each show. Some take all the money prizes and give the owner the trophy. Some make arrangements to have half of the stud fees. Some will give you hints on how to prepare your dog and you pay only handling fee, keeping the dog at home between shows.

I am quite certain you will find most professional breeders and handlers only too willing to give you a great deal of help. After all, it is up to them to encourage new dogs, for they are the backbone of the breed, ready to carry on when the oldsters, of necessity, leave off. To any serious breeder this is important. For surely the breeding of beautiful dogs is not just a thing for now. We must always look to the future, hoping that what we do today will be looked upon in years to come as some small part of the history of our very beautiful breed. So expect the big breeders to be willing to help you, to give you a leg up, to show you if you are making mistakes in your grooming, in your presentation of your dog, even in your handling.

The big all-breed shows are really quite a revelation. For here you will see, not only dogs, but everything pertaining to dogs. It is like a town square on market day. There are stalls offering all kinds of things – dog foods, canned or otherwise, dog crates, beds, collars, leads, chains, brushes and combs and all kinds of grooming tools, and dog coats, from serviceable rainproof ones to very snazzy mink ones. These latter are mainly for poodles and chihuahuas. These breeds too have their own specialty in collars – diamond studded ones, emerald, all kinds in fact, even collars with fur around the edges.

You will find stands for photographers, portrait painters; stalls where you can buy note paper and envelopes with doggy pictures on them; stalls displaying a wide range of chinaware depicting dogs of all breeds and at all activities; stands with a vast number of books pertaining to dogs and doggy subjects; stands which show ranges of kennels, kennel runs; and in fact, as far as dogs are concerned, anything you want, name it and the dog show stands will have it as well as a lot of things you never thought of naming.

In the United States, as I have said, for a dog to become a champion he must obtain 15 points. Sometimes he can only obtain one point at a show. So believe you me, you will often spend so much time before you acquire 15 points, that you will know those little stands inside and out and backwards.

The same is true in Britain, where a dog has to obtain three Challenge Certificates from three different judges to become a champion, and this can take him considerably longer than it does to obtain 15 American points. So British breeders, too, are grateful for these stalls where they can while away idle hours on the long hard path to championship.

Sable and white is the most popular color and usually the most common. The term "sable and white" covers all shades from palest gold to richest mahogany.

XII Breeding the Collie

Heredity

If your original purchase was a bitch puppy, sooner or later you will have to decide whether you want to breed her or not. If your intention was always to do this, then quite probably you selected one with a good pedigree. However, if your puppy was chosen more as a pet than for breeding, you must first of all consider whether it would be in the interests of the breed to allow her to have a litter.

If your bitch has a number of faults, no matter how careful you are in selecting the dog to whom she is to be mated, there is always a chance that you will perpetuate these faults; this would be wrong. Take advice, therefore, from the more experienced breeders as to whether they think she should be mated or not. Some people feel that, in the interests of health, a bitch should have at least one litter in her life. So, if you are advised that this would be good for your Collie, then of course, the question of whether or not to mate her no longer arises. There is only one answer – breed her.

Let us, for the moment, assume that you have a good bitch of good parentage and it is your intention to endeavor to produce prize-winning puppies from her. Before setting out on this hard road, a great deal of thought must be taken – thought about the genetic makeup of your bitch and that of her prospective mate, for without some knowledge of heredity, no one can breed better dogs.

In a book of this scope, one cannot possibly include a treatise on the science of genetics. All I can do is to try to offer you helpful hints, based upon certain genetic laws.

Thinking back to our school days, we learned how every animal, no matter what species, was the result of two cells joining and becoming one. How did this joined cell then divide into two, two into four, four into eight, eight into sixteen, and so on, each cell having its own special job to do, and each cell becoming a different part of the animal – brain, lungs, muscles, tissues, bones, and so forth? Most important of all in a study of heredity are those cells known as germ cells whose jobs it is to make more cells, which in turn become the cells of heredity, passing to the next generation those hereditary traits received from their own parents. All cells die when the animal does, but these germ cells are, in the act of reproduction, passed into the new cell, which in turn becomes a living animal.

That a cell, so tiny a thing that it can be seen only under a microscope, can end up as a living dog, be it Chihuahua or Great Dane, is hard to believe and harder still to believe is that it is only the nucleus within the cell that is the really important part.

The nucleus is composed of a number of tiny bodies. Even under the microscope these tiny bodies are very difficult to see because they look transparent, and the only way to observe them properly is to stain them with dye. They absorb so much color that they become very distinct, and it is for this reason that they are known as chromosomes, or colored bodies. Every animal – be it reptile, insect or man – has a definite number of chromosomes, and the number of chromosomes in each species is constant, for instance, the dog has 39 pairs. Each of these chromosomes is made up of a vast number of tiny units, which we call genes, and to genes we shall return in a moment.

When the bitch is ready for mating, the eggs within her ovaries are ripe. Each ovum, while it is ripening, is contained in a little sac, and when it is ripe, the sac bursts and the ovum is discharged into the area surrounding the ovary.

If the bitch has been mated before the ova are discharged, each ovum will be fertilized by one of the sperm which will be waiting. If, however, the mating has not yet taken place, the ova will have to wait. The life of the ripened ovum, once it is discharged in the ovary, is believed to be very short, and the possibilities are that a number of ova will go to waste and die before encountering a sperm.

At the time of mating, the dog injects semen into the vagina of the bitch. This semen carries the sperm. Many millions are discharged at each emission. It will be seen, therefore, how many are wasted, because only those sperm fortunate enough to encounter a ripe egg are of service. The individual sperm is a self-propelling cell. It has its own method of swimming in the semen. One can best liken the sperm to a minute ball with a long thread-like tail which propels it. When the sperm cell contacts an ovum, it penetrates the outer wall and this wall immediately thickens, making it impervious to any other sperm. The ovum rids itself of half its chromosomes, and the nucleus of the sperm, which is very, very much smaller than that of the ovim, begins to grow on nourishment taken from the body of the ovum, and when the sperm nucleus is the same size as that of the ovum, the two join. Each has half of the necessary number of chromosomes. Now the chromosomes pair off, and a new life is created.

Genes

We have said that the chromosomes are made up of a vast number of genes arranged in a definite pattern or group which can be likened to a string of beads. In corresponding chromosomes, the genes situated in the same place all affect the same characteristic, but they can do so in entirely different ways. Such genes are known as allelic.

While there may be more than two alleles for the same gene no dog can possess more than two alleles for the same gene, having received just one from each of his parents. If the two genes are of the same kind, then a dog will be homozygous for the particular characteristic controlled by them. A gene which can have its full effect only when it is present in duplicate is known as a recessive gene. A dominant gene is one which manages to assert itself, even when its partner from the other chromosome is an allele to it, and a dog cannot transmit his phenotype except that part of it which is controlled by his genotype. In simpler words, *a dog cannot possibly pass on to his children his own acquired characteristics. He can only pass on those characteristics which came to him through his own parents.*

You will see then that each parent gave to each puppy one gene for each characteristic, but they were given in such a way that we cannot possibly tell until after the litter is whelped whether the dog's characteristics are dominant because we cannot see what recessives he inherited from his parents. There are a number of exeptions to this rule, for example, if the dog is a tricolor, we know that the color is recessive. That is the only thing we can be completely sure about, for even a pure golden sable is not necessarily a homozygous sable unless the dog has been tested through a series of matings.

The study of simple genetics is one of great value to the serious breeder. Even if you are not planning to breed seriously, it can be fascinating. It is impossible to go into it at greater length in this book, but there are a vast number of books on the subject, many of them specializing on genetics in the dog, and I can only recommend that you obtain one of these and study it carefully. Unfortunately not enough has been published as yet on heredity in the Collie, and the only thing on which we have really definite knowledge is the inheritance of coat color.

Coat Color Inheritance

The Collie is accepted in four colors – sable and white in all shades; tricolor; blue merle; and in certain countries of the world the pure white with a colored head, the head being either tricolor or sable.

Sable and white: This color is probably the most popular, and usually the most common. The term "sable and white" covers all shades from palest gold to rich mahogany, and nobody quite knows where the apparent misnomer of "sable and brown" came from, but it is, undoubtedly, here to stay. There are two kinds of inheritance in the sable Collie. The more usual is the heterozygous sable which, mated to another sable of his own genetic type, will produce sables in various shades as well as tricolors.

We do, occasionally, get the homozygous sable which no matter whether it is mated to heterozygous sables or to tricolors, can produce nothing but sables. These sables, however, can range from gold to quite dark shades. The tricolor is obviously the least interesting to breed from a genetic point of view because his color is truly recessive. Tricolor mated to tricolor will never produce anything but tricolors. The only variance is in the white markings. The white Collie can be produced from a white factored sable or a white factored tricolor, or, naturally from the white itself. The white Collie mated to a full-color dog can produce either whites or sable or tricolor, according to the color of its partner, but it will only produce white when mated to a full-color dog, if the full-colored animal is white factored.

Blue-merle: The blue merle pattern is a modification of black, owing to the presence of a dilution factor, and to the spread of the granules of pigmentation in each hair. The blue merle does not appear from an alternation of different colored hairs as is the case in the roan,

Tricolor is truly recessive. Tricolor mated to tricolor, therefore, will only produce tricolor. However, it is possible, as we see here, for a tricolor to be born in a litter of sables.

for instance, of Cocker Spaniels or of a horse. It is virtually impossible to produce a blue merle unless one parent is a blue merle. The only exceptions to this are a fairly rare mutation, or long-hidden recessives, which occur when two sables are mated together, each carrying way back in their pedigree a blue merle ancestor. It is then barely possible for each of the animals concerned to be recessive for blue merle, and very, very occasionally a blue puppy will come up in a litter from two such sables. Except for this one instance, it is impossible to produce a blue merle unless the bi-color black and tan pattern is present, for the dilution factor must work on the bi-color to produce true blue merles.

The Mating Season

So you have decided that your bitch is to have a litter. Now it is up to you to see that, at the time her season is due, she is in the best possible health and condition. A prospective brood bitch should never be allowed to grow fat. It is important too that before mating she is free of worms or any parasite; treat her for worms routinely at the first sign of her coming into season.

A bitch comes into season, or heat, at fairly regular intervals. In most breeds these intervals are approximately six months apart, although, in fact, with Collies it is more usual for the interval to be longer, very often ten or twelve months between seasons. The first sign of a bitch coming into heat will probably be noticed when other dogs start to follow her, but if there are no dogs in your household, and you do not meet any when you are out walking, it is up to you to watch her carefully. She may start licking herself, and you will notice a bloody discharge. At this point the season is just beginning, and mating can occur only when this discharge has entirely or almost ceased. The period for cessation varies greatly from bitch to bitch, but it can usually be expected eleven or twelve days after the season's onset.

However, Collie bitches are usually so very clean and fussy about keeping themselves clean during these periods that your bitch may be in season for several days before you are aware of it. For this reason, once you have noticed that she is in season, watch her carefully while waiting for the bloody discharge to cease because if you have already missed counting three, four, even five days, the time for mating will come quicker than you expect.

Again, there is the occasional bitch who comes into season and shows no discharge at all. She is a real problem if she is the only dog, because without the help of a male, it may well be that you will miss her season altogether. However, such bitches are fortunately rare.

The moment you notice the first sign of the bitch's season is the time for you to advise the owner of the male (known as the stud) you have chosen to mate her to, because every stud dog owner likes to have several days' notice in order to organize things at his end. It is extremely difficult when the owner of the stud is phoned in the morning to be told, "My bitch is ready; I want to bring her this afternoon". You may well find, if you leave it to the last minute, that nothing can be arranged and that a mating this time is impossible.

In a number of breeds, an early sign of season is the fact that the vulva becomes enlarged and swollen. Do not wait to see this in a Collie because it is difficult to see, because of the long coat. At the time of a mating, there may appear almost no swelling whatsoever. So do not depend on this. The exact time at which the bitch will accept a stud varies both from breed to breed and from individual to individual. I have known bitches who if they were not mated before the fourth day, never had puppies at all, and others who have been as late as the nineteenth or twentieth day. The bitch herself may vary from season to season. Quite often you will find that when a bitch is young she may need to be mated early in the season, and as she becomes older, she becomes more normal. I have a Collie bitch who once had to be mated always by the sixth day, sometimes as early as the second, but when she was six of seven years old, the twelfth or fourteenth day was the time.

Earlier, I said that it is generally accepted that the correct time for mating is when the red discharge has ceased, but even this is not infallible as there are bitches who will continue to have a red discharge throughout the period of the season so if you wait for it to stop, you will miss your opportunity.

Recent research in the United States has established something which should be extremely helpful to breeders. It has been discovered that when the bitch is at the peak of her season and is fertile, the vagina secretes glucose and at this time only. There is on the market a test paper available for humans suffering from diabetes, which is specific for the presence of glucose only. A test can be made by the introduction of this paper into the bitch's vagina; in the presence of glucose the paper turns green. If this test is made and the paper does not turn green, it is quite useless to waste your time and the dog's energy trying to effect a mating because even if a mating takes place, it will be infertile.

From the onset of the season until you take your bitch to the stud, you must watch her carefully and never let her out alone nor into contact with another dog, so that there can be no chance of a mesalliance. I cannot stress too much the necessity for taking extreme care because, while the bitch is at the peak of her season, not only will she have the natural urge to go seek a male, but also the males around – and you will be surprised how far around – will have a strong natural urge to come seeking her, and what you might well think is a suitable protective barrier turns out, in fact, to be no barrier at all. Dogs will climb in open windows. I have even known a bitch to break one and jump out. They will dig under wire, or leap to almost unimaginable heights to attain the object of their desire. It is wise, if it can be so arranged, not to let the bitch off your premises, because if she does not go outside and does not leave traces of her scent around, the annoyance of visiting suitors will be lessened.

Nowadays it is possible to obtain either chemically scented preparations which are supposed to discourage the male, or drugs to be given internally to remove the scent from the bitch herself. In the first instance I have found that males get used to the scented preparation, and so it has no effect at all. In the second, if you use an internal deodorant, probably chlorophyll, it is essential to stop using it at least 24 hours, preferably 48 hours, before the mating.

If the mating is a normal one, and there is a good "tie" (a word which I will explain further on), there should be no necessity for a second mating, and it is unreasonable to expect the owner of a popular stud to give you one. Do remember, however, that even after your bitch is mated, you must still keep her confined for the remaining period of her heat – and even a little longer to be sure – for it is perfectly possible for a bitch to conceive by two dogs in the same heat period. So if a day or two after having been mated to the dog of your choice, she gets out and mates again, you may well find that she has conceived in both matings, and you will end up with two lots of puppies by different fathers. If the two fathers are of different breeds, you may be able to tell whose puppy is which but this is not always easy. So for everybody's sake, and the reputation of the sire, please be careful to keep your bitch as well confined after she has been mated as before.

At the beginning of the last paragraph I used the word "tie". This is something peculiar to the canine species. No other mammal has to tie during copulation. Although I say "has to tie", it is not always essential for the dog either, but it is natural. In other species the male is equipped with Cowper's glands. These enable the animal to eject the semen in a quick squirt as soon as the vagina is penetrated. The dog does not have these glands and so can only eject his semen on a "grip" principle. But nature has taken good care of things in her inimitable way, and introduced the tie.

When the penis enters the vagina and the dog has worked for a moment or two, the penis enlarges into a large bulbous swelling at its posterior part. This is gripped in the muscles of the vagina, and so the dog is held – or tied – within the bitch for a varying period of time. It can be as short as two or three minutes, it can be as long as an hour, or even two; though these last are rare, thank goodness. The average is from fifteen to twenty minutes. A dog varies tremendously in the lengths of time he is tied to various bitches. While it is possible for puppies to be conceived without there being a tie, in my experience with Collies I have found it extremely rare, and I am never satisfied unless my Collie dog and bitch have, in fact, tied. If the pair are tied for fifteen minutes the semen and sperm will penetrate the entire length of the uterus.

After the mating allow the bitch to rest a little before taking her away. However, if she is travelling with you in your car, and she is used to car travel, there is probably little harm in taking her away at once. If, however, the bitch has been sent away for a mating, and must make the return trip boxed, by air or by rail, then it is very wise to let her rest for a whole night before returning her home.

Once your bitch is home, take the precautions mentioned earlier but, otherwise, treat her normally for the first three weeks – usual exercise, usual diet. There is no reason to alter the diet of a pregnant bitch before the fourth week; by then you should have an inkling of whether or not she is pregnant, or to use the dog world term: in whelp. Keep her clean, of course, but treat her normally.

Should you suspect, at about the third week, that she has worms, it might be wise to seek veterinary advice as to whether it is wise to worm her again at this stage, or not. Very often "not" is the answer.

Before the fourth week after mating, it may not be possible to tell whether or not the bitch is in whelp. With a maiden bitch it may even be considerably longer before there are visual signs. Some veter-

Start weaning your puppies when they are three weeks old. They should be thoroughly weaned between five and six weeks of age – but sometimes they just don't seem to know it.

inarians may be able, between the 21st and 28th day, and only between these days, to tell you whether or not your bitch is, in fact, in whelp. This they can do by palpating. Any other signs are those which will be apparent only to you because you know her so well: changes in character, changes in habit, and, possibly, an erratic appetite – eating one day voraciously, and refusing everything the next.

From the fourth week onwards, however, you must increase the bitch's food ration, especially so if the vet has told you that she is in whelp. The diet of the pregnant bitch has already been discussed in the chapter on feeding.

Aside from increasing the diet, there is nothing to do during these nine weeks of waiting, except to be sure that the bitch gets plenty of exercise. During the early days, this can be just as it is normally, but she should never be forced to take a walk by dragging her along if she does not want to go. In the beginning, she will probably behave just as usual: chasing birds, other dogs, or whatever she has enjoyed doing in her normal routine, and nothing should be done to alter this. However, if normally she is exercised with other boisterous dogs, do not continue this because she might get an accidental bump that could harm her or the puppies. During the later stages of pregnancy, she should be taken out either alone or with one staid elderly dog to keep her company. Some breeders feel that in the last week of pregnancy a bitch should be exercised only on a leash. This I try to avoid, because then she might be forced to take more exercise than she wants. If she is allowed to run free, she will soon let you know when she is ready to go home.

There is one other thing that requires attention – her bowel movements. She should never become constipated. In fact, the bowel movements of a pregnant bitch should be more frequent than normally because she has not only to get rid of her own wastes but also those of her unborn puppies. If your bitch appears constipated, she must be given some kind of laxative, but a drug at this stage would be dangerous. Mineral oil is a safe remedy, but it should not be used too often because it depletes the vitamin reserves. Being an oil it absorbs the oil-soluble vitamins, so that while an occasional dose is perfectly safe, it must never be used with regularity. The dose for a Collie is about a soupspoonful it can be poured over a meal because it is both odorless and tasteless. However, if your Collie shows signs of constipation, ask yourself this question, has she always had plenty of fresh water? Drinking water is a natural help to bowel action, and please, never, never forget it.

The Whelping Box

When the bitch is five or six weeks in whelp, it is time to make

At times it may be necessary to supplement the mother's feeding, particularly if she has an exceedingly large litter.

arrangements for her whelping quarters; it is always advisible to accustom her to these some time before the puppies are due. The set-up depends, of course, on whether she is going to whelp in a warm room, outside in a kennel, or under the heat of an infrared lamp. If she is to whelp outside in a kennel, she should have an enclosed box, with a lid for your own convenience, and an adequately sized hole through which she can go easily in and out; hang a blanket across the hole to keep the heat inside.

If she is to whelp in the house, or under an infra-red lamp, she can have an open box, some three feet by four, with sides up to one foot high. If the sides are high, one end should be constructed so that it can be hinged up or down, then later when the puppies are big enough to move around, they can be kept in or out as desired.

It is a wise precaution, too, to put a guard rail inside the box to keep the puppies from being squashed against the sides by their mother. This rail should be approximately three or four inches from the bottom – just high enough for a baby puppy to crawl underneath out of harm's way. Do not think from this that the mother is naturally clumsy. She is not. You will be amazed how careful she can be the Collie, even with a large litter, is so clever about arranging her nest that she rarely sits on or harms a puppy in any way.

Undoubtedly the best bedding for a whelping box is newspaper; it is absorbent, and when it becomes dirty, it can be quickly and cheaply replaced. There is, I understand, a limited amount of disinfectant in newsprint, so this makes it even more acceptable. In fact, only on two occasions in all the years that I have been breeding dogs, have I had puppies with infected umbilicals. On both these unhappy occasions I had used blankets instead of newspapers because the weather was excessively cold and I felt the puppies needed the extra warmth. Even though the blankets were spotlessly clean, the puppies became infected. I swore then and there never again to rear newborn puppies on anything except newspaper.

Some people use straw, but I am against it because a puppy can easily get lost under the straw, or, in an extreme case, damage an eye by running its head on to a stiff stalk. Hay is not advisable either because it has a tendency to harbor fleas and other parasites.

Personal Hygiene

Certain preparations must be made for the bitch herself. About ten days before the puppies are due, cut off all hair on her abdomen, especially around the teats. It is also a wise precaution to cut off her petticoats, and if she has very long hair on the underside of her tail, remove this too. I know of a puppy that got caught in this long hair, and broke its neck when the mother tried to get up.

While it is generally accepted that the time of gestation is 63 days, in practice you will find 61 days much more likely, especially if yours is a maiden bitch. Therefore, at the 58th or 59th day, examine her teats and remove any dirt adhering to them. Continue to keep her teats clean until the puppies are born.

Although a bitch will frequently whelp in less than 63 days, it is also possible that she will go over the normal period, and this is something I do not like. If a bitch of mine is more than 24 hours late, I anticipate danger, and take veterinary advice,

Signs of Labor

The first sign that a bitch is going into labor may well be just a general restlessness. She may not let you out of her sight; she may, on the other hand, want to be alone, although this is unlikely. This period of general unrest may last for as long as two days, but it is as well when it begins to prepare for things to happen. She should, of course, have been introduced to her whelping box some time before, and now, if you think the birthdate near, take her to it. If necessary, remain with her, because she may, as I have said, not want to be alone. She will soon show signs of wishing to make a nest. This she will do by tearing up the paper, both by scrabbling at it with her feet and by tearing with her mouth, until she has, as she hopes, arranged things the way she wants them. It is, of course, up to you to disarrange them and to give her new paper just as often as she tears up the old, because if she is left at the moment of whelping with mounds of torn paper in her box, she may end up with a puppy lost under the mountain.

Some time before labor actually starts, probably a matter of hours, the vagina and vulva begin to soften and discharge a white mucus. A bitch who has already had a litter may well start secreting milk several days before the puppies are born. But with a maiden bitch the milk often does not show itself until the whole litter has been born, so there is no need, in the early hours, to concern yourself about its absence.

There is one sure and certain sign that a bitch is going into labor;

this is a drop in her temperature. We noted earlier that the normal temperature of a dog is about 101.5° F. Some 24 hours before the onset of labor, a bitch's temperature will start to drop, usually to as low as 99° F., sometimes even less. I have known one whose temperature always went down to 94° F. twenty-four hours before the onset of labor. If, from about the 56th day after mating, you take the temperature rectally, night and morning, you will have a pretty good guide as to when the puppies are likely to appear. This may well save you several sleepless nights, for there is no need to become anxious until you have noted this drop in temperature.

The Whelping

If your bitch is fit, healthy and normal, her whelping should be normal too. I do not intend to deal with the abnormalities of whelping, but to give you an idea of what to expect and how to deal with it.

Each puppy is born separately, attached by its umbilical to an individual afterbirth, or placenta. During its time in the uterus, the placenta was attached to the wall and this is how the puppy obtained its nourishment and oxygen. At the moment of birth, the placenta detaches from the uterine wall and the puppy begins life on its own.

Each puppy is contained in its own sac, which surrounds the puppy with a fluid that acts protectively to shield it from damaging blows or pressure, and at birth becomes the means of dilating the birth canal and lubricating it.

When the mother starts to labor, a series of irregular contractions of the uterine muscle begins. These are neither rhythmical nor powerful in the early stages, and they are not visible to the eye, but their job is to bring on the relaxation and dilation of the lower part of the uterus and of the vagina, to enable the puppies to be born with ease. It is these early contractions that cause our bitch to become restless, to pant, to be obviously uncomfortable and in pain. It is impossible to give a time limit for this first stage. It may last only a few hours; it may last a day or more, but it is not until it has been completed, and the dilation taken place, that the second stage of labor – the one we can see begins.

Now, the contractions become both obvious and regular, and the bitch strains to gradually force the puppy down the birth canal. Between each contraction she will rest and pant. The sign that the puppy is about to be born is when there is very little rest and panting and the contractions follow one another quickly and powerfully, slowly forcing the first puppy out of the uterus, through the vagina and into the world.

Normally, the first thing to appear is the little sac in which the puppy is enclosed. This may still be unbroken with the puppy and the fluid inside, or while it is travelling down the vagina, it may rupture and expel the fluid; it is this rupturing of the sac that heralds the coming of the puppy.

About fifty percent of all puppies are born head first with their chins resting on their front legs. I have found, however, that almost as many Collie puppies are born hind legs first. This presentation is, possibly, even easier than a frontal one.

The Umbilical Cord and Sac

No matter whether the puppy comes head or hind legs first, it will be expelled with its umbilical cord still attached. It is possible that the placenta will, at the very beginning, still be retained inside the mother, and so the cord will appear to go back into her as well. But if the contractions have been sufficiently strong, the puppy and the placenta will be expelled closely together. If the sac has not been broken, the first thing the bitch should do is to tear it apart and get the puppy's head out. If she fails to do this, you must do it immediately.

Puppies inside the dam do not breathe; they obtain all the oxygen they need through the placenta and the uterine wall from the blood of the mother. The moment the placenta is detached from the uterine wall, this supply of oxygen is cut off. Now the little puppy must obtain its own oxygen by breathing, so it is essential that the sac be ruptured to let the puppy fill its lungs with air. This sac can easily be broken with the fingers, and once it is done, nothing else is urgently essential, so there need be no panic.

However, with a maiden bitch, it is possible that she will lack the instinct to tell her what to do, and so you must take this first puppy, break the cord (I will tell you how in a minute), and dry the puppy, rubbing it rather roughly with a coarse towel until it cries, and the moment it cries, almost certainly its mother will say, "Give it to me quick! It's mine!" and from that moment she will take over.

The mother should bite the umbilical cord, severing the puppy from the afterbirth, which she should eat. If she fails to sever the cord, it is up to you to do it for her. This is not a matter of great urgency, and there is no need to panic about it. Take the puppy in your hand, and squeeze the cord flat about one inch from the body; wait for a few moments until the circulation has ceased, pressing the cord tightly between your thumb and first finger. Then cut the cord with scissors, cutting, of course, on the side of your fingers away from the puppy. This obviates the necessity of tying the cord with thread, but if you prefer to tie it, you may. Immediately give the puppy back to its mother, who should then busily lick it dry.

Intervals Between Puppies

To be definite about the time lapse between the birth of each puppy is impossible. It varies greatly; even the same bitch will have different intervals between different puppies; but once the first puppy is born, you can usually expect the second to arrive fairly soon, maybe even before the mother has finished drying the first one. The intervals may vary from a matter of minutes to half an hour, or even a full hour, and it is quite usual for a bitch with a largish litter to have a long rest halfway through. This rest may last for an hour or several hours. If she is really resting and not straining, there is no need to worry. However, if she strains and pants for a long time and appears to be in pain, particularly if the contractions are short and very severe, this is almost a certain indication of trouble, possibly of obstruction by one puppy which has been malpositioned. For this, your vet must immediately be alerted, as it is a time for professional assistance.

It is not always easy to tell when the last puppy has been born. Therefore, it is probably wise to ask your veterinarian to stop by anyway when you think the births have been completed, so that he may check your bitch and make sure that no puppy or afterbirth has been retained.

During the actual period of whelping the bitch may be offered milk from time to time. Many breeders say this milk should be warm; in my opinion, it should be cold, for, particularly, in the case of a large litter or a fairly long whelping, warm milk tends to make the bitch sleepy, and it is likely to calm down the uterine contractions. Iced or cold milk is much more likely to keep her awake and alert. If she appears completely exhausted, a teaspoonful or so of brandy may work to her advantage, but an exhausted bitch is rare because she is usually stimulated by the arrival of her puppies, and will give you no bother at all.

There is, however, no doubt in my mind that a bitch likes to have you remain with her while her babies are being born. Even if there is nothing for you to do, the very fact that you are beside her, I am quite certain, gives her confidence. Furthermore, it will ease your own mind because you will know that everything is going according to plan, and there is nothing to worry about.

We have talked about a bitch having her proper whelping quarters and becoming accustomed to them, but occasionally you will find a bitch who absolutely insists on having her puppies in a certain spot, and nothing you can do will make her alter her mind. It is up to you you to accommodate such a contrary lady and make the best of a bad job – if that is what it is for you. I know of one particular bitch – not a Collie, however – whose owner was determined that she would have her puppies in a box in the bathroom; the bitch was equally determined to have them on the drawing room sofa. Every time the bitch started in labor on the sofa, her owner put her in the bathroom, whereupon the bitch stopped her straining until she was allowed to return to the drawing room. Unfortunately, the owner was even more determined than the bitch, and insisted that she should whelp in the bathroom. The result – the bitch refused to produce her puppies at all and the owner lost the entire litter, and nearly the mother as well.

Eating the Afterbirth

Returning to the subject of the bitch's eating the afterbirth, there are two schools of thought on this. Some breeders stand by and take away each afterbirth as it is severed, not allowing the bitch to eat them. In my opinion this is a grave mistake. In the wild state, the afterbirth provided food for the mother because she was unlikely to be able to hunt for two or three days after the puppies were born, and the afterbirth provided her with needed nourishment. It contains many beneficial nutriments, and also acts as a laxative. Further, there is something in the afterbirth that makes a bitch more motherly.

No, this is not your puppy, although the little Chihuahua is not much bigger.

XIII   Caring for the Litter

When the whelping has been completed, get an assistant to take the bitch outside for a few minutes to relieve herself while you move the puppies, completely renew the bedding, and put them back in bed before the mother returns. Then give her a drink of milk – warm, this time – and leave another bowl of milk in the box with her. Then leave her quietly to sleep and rest, because she will need this; but look in from time to time to make sure that no puppy has been pushed away, and is not getting his fair share of milk, or is running a risk of being chilled. With a maiden bitch, as I have said, the milk does not always become apparent until the puppies have started to suckle, and it may sometimes be several hours after the birth before milk appears. A newborn puppy can exist for as long as 24 hours without suckling, if necessary, but it is absolutely essential that it be kept warm. Many more puppies die from chills than from starvation. If necessary, it is always possible to give a puppy a supplementary feed while waiting for the bitch's milk to be secreted, and this feed can be given either with a premature-baby bottle or by the new method of tube feeding which I am about to describe.

Emergency Feeding

In an emergency, it may be necessary to supplement the mother's milk. Cows' milk alone won't do it. There is a great variation between "dog" milk and "cow" milk. The bitch's milk contains more fat and protein, and less sugar. Old formulas recommended adding lime water, glucose or dextrose. Today we know that there is no need. There are on the market various brands of prepared dry-milk foods formulated for whelps. If one is not available at your pet shop, try one of the spray-dried milks prepared for human babies. Mix one part of the preparation in six parts of water, and add one part of light cream. A quantity can be prepared and kept refrigerated. It must, of course, be warmed and shaken before it is fed to the puppies.

If time is of the essence, and it is impossible to obtain a commercially prepared dry food, then regular cows' milk can be used *but* add one part of beaten egg yolk (be absolutely sure there is no white) to each four parts of cows' milk – this will enrich it with the needed protein so important to early growth.

It is not necessary to use a special premature baby bottle or pet feeding bottle after the puppy is 2 weeks old. They will suck freely on a regular baby nurser.

LOUISE VAN DER MEID

Tube Feeding

This is a new way to feed tiny puppies, not too often known by breeders; once mastered there is no easier, safer or quicker method.

Required are a small catheter (size 21), a 10 CC syringe, and a spring hair-clip to act as a clamp. It is perhaps better for the novice to ask a veterinarian how to tube-feed a puppy for the first time. It is a delicate matter of putting the tube down the throat and making certain it goes into the stomach and not into the air passage.

Before each feed the catheter and syringe should be placed in cold water and boiled for three minutes. The formula used should be at blood temperature. Attach the catheter to the nozzle of the syringe and draw up the contents of the formula. Press the piston of the syringe until the milk goes through the catheter and then clamp the catheter a few inches from the end. Dip the end in the milk mixture, so that it is appetizing.

The easiest way to feed is to stand the puppy on a table covered with a rough towel. Hold the puppy with the left hand across the back and neck, open the mouth with the thumb and first finger of the left hand, and insert the catheter with the right hand, pushing it a little at a time down the throat. The puppy usually helps by conveniently swallowing. If the puppy gags, or the tube does not go down easily, it is probably not correctly positioned and is entering the air passage. Pull it up and start again.

It is important to keep the puppy's head *down and forward* while inserting the tube; never up or back. For the novice to make quite certain that the tube is correctly inserted it is probably better not to attach the syringe to the tube but to clamp the end, or to place a small stopper in it. As soon as the tube is in the stomach, unclamp the end and place it under water in a cup. If the water bubbles, the tube is in the air passage and must be withdrawn at once. If there are no bubbles all is well. Attach the syringe, remove the clamp and press on the piston with the thumb of the right hand. The stomach will start to swell with the mixture, and when there is still a little give to the stomach, the puppy will have had enough.

When the syringe is removed, take out the tube and clean the puppy. It is absolutely essential to wash the equipment immediately after each meal, flushing out the catheter with the syringe several times. Before each meal the syringe and the catheter should be dismantled and placed in cold water and boiled for three minutes.

How Often to Feed

The question of how often to tube-feed a nursing puppy is a moot one. The latest findings are that a puppy can be fed by this method. as infrequently as every six hours. If this is the case, then the first feed of the day should be at 6 a.m., and later feeds at six-hour intervals. Six hours, however, may be too long for some tiny puppies to go without a feed; the best way to ascertain this is to see how long your puppy will go between meals, sleeping and not crying. If he starts to cry, he is probably hungry, so let this mark the length of time between feeds.

Care of the Weak Puppy

The first few days in the life of a puppy are desperately important. Look at your litter every few hours, day and night, during these first days, because if you spot early that a puppy is being pushed away and becoming chilled, you can save it, but if it is left untended for several hours, you have very little chance of doing so. And again, if your puppy is not getting his fair share at the milk bar, and is being pushed away by the others, and you spot this at once, you can probably save his life by giving him a supplementary feed, whereas if he has already become so starved that he is too weak to suckle, your task is far harder, and may well be fruitless.

When I open the door of the whelping room, I like to hear one of three things: either dead silence, shrieking hungry noises, or contented suckling. The first denotes that your puppies have fed and are sound asleep and happy; the second, that you have arrived just as feeding time is due and they are all awake because they are hungry; the third, that you have arrived just as feeding time has started, and those gorgeous contented suckling noises are a sure sign that everybody is doing well. The noise I do not like to hear is one that sounds like a kitten mewing or a gull screaming. This is a sign that you have a weak puppy who is doing badly, who is starved or chilled; this is the sound you must listen for and on hearing take immediate action.

If you find a puppy chilled or unhappy, take it away at once. A word of warning here: the mother will probably be very concerned if she sees you making off with a puppy, so pick up two puppies together, replacing one quickly beside her, and hiding the other so that she does not realize you still have it. Then go off with it. If it is chilled and cold, wrap it first in a blanket or towel then put it in a warm oven – with the door left open, obviously – or in the warming drawer of your oven, and leave it there for some time. You will be astonished how a puppy, warmed this way, will revive, will be strong the next time you look at it, and who, frequently, after one supplementary feed can be returned to its mother, never to need extra attention again. If, however, you find that the same puppy is always being pushed away, do your very best for it. Make a point of going back at least every two hours and holding it to the nipple to nurse. You will find that after a day or so of this treatment the puppy will probably perk up and be well able to take care of itself in the general rough and tumble of litter feeding. This rough and tumble is, in fact, essential because it provides the puppies with the necessary exercise to keep them fit.

If you are only giving an occasional supplementary feed, the mother will look after the puppies, keeping them warm and clean, but if for some reason – the death of the mother perhaps – you find that you are left with an entire litter to hand-feed, there is a great deal more to do than just feed. First of all, there is the problem of keeping the puppies warm, and second, after every feed you must do something to approximate the action of their mother's tongue. After every meal the puppy's belly must be gently rubbed with olive oil until the puppy has both a bowel and bladder movement. The puppy must be kept clean by wiping the anus, and the vulva or the penis, with clean cotton wrung out in a little bit of disinfectant after each movement; its face must always be kept clean as well. It is necessary to dry the puppy afterwards, and, if desired, the anus can be sprinkled with a little boracic or talcum powder. Hand-feeding by bottle or tube should be continued with measurably longer intervals between feeds until the puppies are about 2-1/2 weeks old; then you can start to wean them to solid foods, as I have discussed in an earlier chapter.

It is essential to remember when hand-feeding puppies, that everything should be sterilized and kept just as clean as when feeding human babies.

You will find that a good mother is most reluctant ever to leave her litter, not even wanting to go out to relieve herself. I never make a bitch leave her puppies for the first 24 hours after the birth, unless she herself shows that she wants to, but after 24 hours I do make her go. It will probably be necessary to put on a lead to get her out of

At six weeks of age, a puppy is ready for adoption.

the box, and then she should be taken into the yard and left there for a few minutes. She will soon come to the door yelping, when she should be allowed to go back to her puppies. During the time she has been out, you will, of course, have had an opportunity to change the bedding, making sure that everything is as it should be. As the days pass, she will be quite happy to spend longer spells away from her babies, and if she is a good mother she should be encouraged to do so, because so many Collies give too much of themselves to their litters, and it is rare to find one who will willingly neglect her puppies. However, there is one thing of which to beware. Never, as long as a bitch is nursing a litter, allow her to go out and chase and race with other dogs, for this tends to dry up her milk quickly, and too much excitement and exercise can cause a calcium deficiency which may result in fits.

For me, the ideal is to have my bitch in the house for the first three or four days after the puppies are born. Then I put her and the litter into a kennel with a run and give her constant access to this run. If she is a good mother, she will rarely be seen in it, only going out when she really needs to. If she seems too anxious to leave

Style in dogs can vary around the world, just as it can in clothing. Collies in Germany, where this picture was taken, are not as a rule as heavy-boned and heavy-coated as they are in the United States and Britain.

her babies, she can easily be shut into the kennel and allowed out only when you deem it wise.

For the first 24 or 36 hours after the whelping, the bitch should be allowed no solid food; simply give her plenty of milk, with the possible addition of an egg and/or a little gruel. If she is perfectly fit at the end of 36 hours, her normal diet as it was at the peak time of her pregnancy may gradually be resumed to reach its maximum within the next three days. The addition of fat to her milk foods for the first two days is a definite advantage because it will restore a great deal of the energy which the whelping has drained from her.

Feeding the Nursing Bitch

One cannot be definite about the quantity to be given during lactation, because this will vary according to the number of puppies. A bitch with four puppies will obviously not need as much food as one with eight or nine. This additional food should be high in protein content, and the bitch should continue her supplement of cod liver oil and calcium. Nor can I stress too often the absolute necessity of always having water present, for nothing will cause the milk supply to dry up more quickly than the lack of fresh water.

Bitch's milk is high in fat content so the addition of 20 % fat to her diet will spare her from using the stored fat in her body.

Comparison of Cow and Bitch Milk

	Fat	Protein	Carbohydrate
Cow	4.0	3.8	4.9
Bitch	11.2	5.7	3.1

Feeding the Baby Puppies

After a normal whelping, the puppies should obtain all the milk they need from their mother. The milk secreted in those early hours is very rich in fats, vitamins and proteins, and it contains many antibodies which will not be present later. During these first several days the antibodies, contained in what is called colostrum, enter the bloodstream of the puppy and give it temporary protection from disease-causing bacteria. After the first few days colostrum is no longer

Collies are long lived, remaining vigorous even at advanced ages. This elegant Collie is 12 years old, but you could never tell that just by looking at him.

available, so if the puppies do not receive it then, their chances of surviving are not quite so great. If for some reason you have to remove one or more puppies from the dam immediately after birth, and she has milk, try to take some of it from her and feed it to your puppy.

Let us assume, however, that all has gone well. If the litter is a large one, it would be of great help both to the puppies and their mother to give them supplementary food as early as the second day. This can be done fairly easily by giving each puppy a bottle-feed once or twice every 24 hours in addition to what it gets from the mother. For this, use a premature baby nipple or a nurser made for pets. There are commercial preparations obtainable at your pet shop which can be substituted for bitchs' milk. As cows' milk is lower in protein and fat but higher in lactose, its use may cause severe diarrhea. Other than this, with a normal litter there is no need to interfere with nature before the puppies are 2½ weeks old.

You have only to watch a two-week old litter to realize just how much energy puppies use up every day – squeaking, squirming, suckling, sleeping, twitching, they keep going all the time. From this it is obvious that their food should be very high in energy producing content. Some breeders start to wean their puppies onto supplementary milk feeds, but I have found it much more beneficial to start the puppy on raw scraped lean meat, for he is almost certainly getting all the milk he needs from his mother.

A puppy at the age of weaning, of no matter what breed, needs about twice as much food per day as when he is grown – pound for pound, of course. It is almost impossible to overfeed a newborn puppy being reared on a suitable diet and getting plenty of exercise; puppies growing up together, with plenty of room to play, will undoubtedly get plenty of exercise.

The structure of any animal depends upon its bone formation, so you must remember that now is the time to feed for good bone. Calcium can easily be obtained in two ways – either in bone flour, or meal, which is a product made from bones or, with a great deal more satisfaction and fun for the puppy, by giving him raw bones to chew, but this, of course, cannot happen until later when the puppy's teeth are well-formed. Bone flour is also an extremely good source of phosphorous, but to enable the dog to assimilate both these minerals correctly, the presence of Vitamin D is essential.

Food supplements are readily obtainable under various trade names, and it is well to ask a dog-owning friend or your veterinarian to recommend one. Since the vitamin and mineral intake must be adequate, some kind of commercial additive may be used if the owner prefers. However, none of these need be added to good commercial foods which contain plenty of calcium phosphorus and vitamins. I mention these additives only in the event you are preparing your own diets. There are available some excellent puppy foods complete in all respects. Many Collie breeders prefer them.

In my estimation, however, your puppy's first supplementary feed should be a solid one of raw meat, so you will want to know how much to give him. The first day, when he is about three weeks old, give him a heaped teaspoonful of scraped raw meat in two separate feedings. To begin with, you will probably have to put it in his mouth to give him the taste. It will be almost no time before he is snatching it out of your fingers, maybe even taking a bite of finger, too. After two days on raw lean meat, other foods can be introduced – liver, any kind of flesh, fish, cheese, dog meal, breadcrumbs, and gradually, more milk plus, as I have said before, vitamin and mineral additives.

When first weaning your puppy you will have to put a little food in his mouth to give him the taste. It will be almost no time before he is snatching it out of your fingers.

LOUISE VAN DER MEID

All food should be slightly warm, about the temperature of the milk the pup receives from its mother – somewhere in the region of 100° F. The only exception to this rule is the bowl of fresh, cool drinking water which should be available from the moment the puppy is able to get on his feet and wander around. Do not rely upon his being able to reach mother's bowl – it may be too high for him. Place a flat dish in the puppies' box so that they can reach it with the greatest of ease.

When you start supplementary feeding separate the puppies from their mother gradually, so that when they are four weeks old she will need to be with them only during the night. The puppies by now will be receiving four or five meals every day. These meals vary, of course; they are discussed in detail in Chapter V.

Dewclaws

All puppies are born with dewclaws – at least dewclaws on the front legs. Very few puppies are born with dewclaws on the hind legs, but if they do appear they must most certainly be removed; this should be done when the puppies are three or four days old by a veterinarian. Removing the dewclaws from the front legs is entirely a matter of choice. There are breeders who think it wise to do so because of the risk later in life of a dewclaw being torn and causing pain. However, I have found this to happen so rarely that I prefer to take the risk and leave the front dewclaws on, and not cause unnecessary pain to a puppy. If you do decide to have the front dewclaws removed, again I advise you to have it done, at least for the

171

first time, by a professional. It is not difficult to do but you must know how to do it.

Other than this, your babies will need very little attention for the first three weeks of their lives. Clean beds; watching that "mom" is happy, well-fed and contented; watching that babies are warm and obviously well-fed; and never forgetting to leave those bowls of fresh water with mother – is really all that you need to worry about until such time as you start to wean the puppies, and this we discuss further on.

Difficult Births

Having dealt fairly extensively with a typical whelping, we should consider briefly some of the things that may go wrong, and I stress that word "may" because I do not wish you to become alarmed or despondent; it is rare for a Collie to have other than a perfectly normal whelping.

First then, do remember that if the sixty-third day arrives and there has been no sign of your bitch's going into labor, do not let more than one more day pass without taking professional advice. To me this is one of the gravest things that can happen to a bitch – that she should go over time; it is *always* a danger signal!

If a bitch in the final stages of labor strains and strains without producing any sign of a puppy, there is obviously something wrong. If, after about an hour and a half, no signs show other than the straining, contact your veterinarian at once, for there may be an obstruction, either a physical obstruction within the bitch or, much more likely, a puppy has been either wrongly presented or is too large to pass through a normal pelvis.

It is impossible for an amateur to diagnose the cause. This is a job for the veterinarian. If the puppy is wrongly presented, it may be possible for the vet to manipulate it into the correct position, and a normal birth will follow. If, however, this is not possible, then obviously the only answer is to perform a Caesarean operation. This is no longer an operation of great gravity; it is one which can be performed without fear provided always that the decision to perform it is taken before the bitch becomes entirely exhausted.

It is, of course, not only with the birth of the first puppy that such an obstruction can occur. A bitch can have three or four puppies perfectly normally, and then will come this delay and straining with no result. Again, the puppy is too large or being wrongly presented, and once again diagnosis must be made by a professional.

If you are a novice breeder, and this is your first litter, forget the "do-it-yourself" bit and send for your veterinarian at once. Do not try to examine your bitch yourself, because in so doing you are almost certain to cause sepsis, and this can only make things more difficult if an operation becomes essential.

The Kiss of Life

While you, as an amateur, can do little to help your bitch if she is having a difficult whelping, there is still a great deal you can do to help a puppy born in a weak condition, or one which will not start to breathe. We have already spoken of warmth for a newborn puppy. The moment it is out of its sac you must make quite certain that there is no mucus in the air passages. A great deal can be done

International Champion Noranda Daily Double. This elegant sable and white rough Collie has been Best in Show, all breeds, twice at shows where there were over 1,000 dogs. Forty-seven judges have awarded him best rough Collie 61 times. He was bred by his owners, Mr. and Mrs. William H. Long, Jr. of Noranda Kennels, Oyster Bay, New York, who have owned his direct line for 20 generations.

by giving the puppy the "kiss of life" (mouth to mouth resuscitation) but obviously this must be done gently with a small amount of breath. It is useless, however, to give the kiss of life if the puppy still has mucus in the air passages. Place the puppy back downwards in the palm of your hand. Put its head between your first and second fingers, holding it firmly around the neck with these two fingers, so that the head does not bounce by itself; then, taking your arm at full length, swing it in a downward direction. It is amazing how hard you can swing, and do the puppy nothing but good, so long as its head is held. As your arm swings down, you may see spots of moisture on the floor; this is a good sign because it means that the mucus is coming out of the air passages. At this moment you can give the kiss of life, and the instant the puppy makes some attempt to breathe by himself rub him briskly with a turkish towel, for the sooner he cries, the more likely he is to live.

Toenails

There is just one more thing you must do for the puppies before weaning time. Frequently one hears the complaint: "Oh, the bitch

By the end of the fourth week you should be giving each puppy at least four ounces of food every day.

won't suckle her puppies. She does nothing but nip at them and tries to get away". Almost always this is the fault of the owner, who has forgotten to cut the puppies' toenails. Puppy toenails are needle-sharp, and digging and pulling on mother when they are feeding causes her a great deal of discomfort. You have only to look at the belly of a bitch whose puppies have not had their toenails cut; you will see it scratched as if by rose thorns; naturally she is in pain. Therefore, make sure that you cut your puppies' toenails at least once a week from the time of birth until they start to run around. I do not find, as a rule, that it is necessary to cut their nails after they start to run around, but in some breeds, and possibly even in some strains of Collie, it is essential to continue to cut toenails during the life of the dog.

At some age in the puppy's life it must be wormed, and I vaguely say "at some age" because here again you should seek the advice of your veterinarian as the vermifuge to be used depends on the age of the puppy. More puppies have been killed by worming than by being left un-wormed, so this is another point on which you should seek professional advice before attempting "do it yourself" methods.

Weaning the Puppies

With a normal, healthy bitch who looks after her babies well, there is nothing for you to do, which I have not already suggested, until such time as the puppies are about three weeks old. At this age, particularly if the litter is a large one, or the bitch is young, it is time for you to help her feed them. The first natural meal of wild puppies consists of their mother's vomit. A female wolf catches her prey which she eats and partially digests. Returning home she re-gurgitates some of it. The food may consist of, perhaps, a whole rabbit including the stomach contents. It is acidified and to us has an obnoxious odor, but puppies like it. They eat all they can and the mother eats the rest and cleans her puppies.

Now I'm not going to suggest that you try to concoct any such meal for your puppies because we have learned from experience and study that some scraped meat will suffice for the first meals, or some baby puppy food made for the purpose by a conscientious manufacturer.

You cannot expect puppies to know what to do the very first time that you offer them food, so you will have to feed each puppy separately. For the first day or two do it with your fingers, pushing the scraped or strained meat, a little bit at a time, into each puppy's mouth. It takes a remarkably short time for the babies to accustom themselves to this delicacy, and they will soon be licking the bits off your fingers.

At this time too, you will start to separate the puppies from their mother for a longer and longer period each day. On the second day, they can have two soupspoonsful of food in two different meals. On the third day you can increase each of these meals to a tablespoonful at a time and by the end of the fourth or fifth day, you can give each puppy one or two ounces of scraped meat or puppy food daily, depending on what age you started to wean them.

By the end of the fourth week, you should be giving each puppy at least four ounces of food every day, and quite probably you will have been able to introduce them to some kind of kibble or fine dog meal scalded and soaked in meat stock, if you care to do so, as I have described in Chapter V.

By the time the puppies are six weeks old, they should be on a schedule of five meals a day, and, at this point, not getting milk from their mother. By now they should not even need her at night. However, if it is a winter litter, reared outside, you will need to keep the kennel warm, especially at night, if their mother is not there to warm them.

Don't forget, though, when taking the mother away, that she still, almost certainly, loves her babies dearly, and will look forward to a short playtime with them, morning and evening. Collie bitches are very devoted, and love romping with their babies, and while you are being kind to her by protecting her from their constant demands, it would be cruel not to allow her regular times with them every day. If you keep any of the puppies she will probably want to play with them for many, many months. I had one bitch who, even when her son was a year old, would "top-and-tail" him every morning, particularly in the car if we were on our way to a show!

From the moment the puppies are able to crawl out of their box, you will, of course, provide them with plenty of fresh, cold water. This water should be renewed at least twice daily, preferably four times. Also remember to add, if you are not sure of the completeness of the diet, food supplements you, or your veterinarian, may consider necessary.

The two or three weeks that elapse between the time the puppies are weaned and sold are of the utmost importance, for in these few

By the time the puppies are six weeks old they should not even need their mother at night. Don't forget, though, when taking the mother away, that she still, almost certainly, loves her babies dearly and will look forward to a short playtime with them, morning and evening.

weeks, the foundations are laid for the rest of their lives. It is then you begin to build the structure of what we hope will develop into a truly beautiful Collie.

Ear Carriage

There is another point to which attention must be paid in these early weeks, and for several months thereafter. This is the ear carriage of your Collie.

The way the mature Collie carries his ears is very important. According to the Breed Standard, the ears should, in repose, be folded lengthwise and thrown back into the frill. On the alert, they are drawn well up on the back skull and are carried about three-quarters erect, with the other quarter of the ear "breaking" forward. This is known as "Tulip ear".

Collie ears present a great many problems, and Collies whose ears are allowed to stay pricked have, in the first place, no value whatsoever as show dogs; they also lose the sweet expression which is part and parcel of the makeup of a good Collie. It is not often that a puppy's ears will stand straight up before he is eight weeks old, but if they do, don't let any time pass before taking action. It is easy to keep your Collie's ears correct if you spot the first sign of faulty ear carriage and deal with it, rather than to let the ears go erect and then have to work on relaxing the muscles.

If a puppy's ear stands up and remains up for more than a few hours, take some olive oil and rub it gently on the tip of the inside of the ear – or better still, a little kaolin; apply it to the inner side of the top third of the ear, and then to avoid its being sticky dust it with talcum powder. This can be repeated as often as necessary. Kaolin can be easily removed with warm water; however, there is

Champion Antrum's All Alone is shown here winning Best of Variety at Pasadena Kennel Club in 1966. This bitch has beautiful head qualities, including smoothness of muzzle and correct eye placement. She has excellent conformation and outstanding showmanship. It is not surprising that she completed her championship before the age of 2, and has wins from California to New York. Champion Antrum's All Alone's lucky owners are Dr. and Mrs. W. H. Hornaday of Los Angeles.

one snag about its use. If you are dealing with one puppy among others, the other pups just love its sweet taste; frequently you will find that no sooner have you put it on than a playmate has licked it off! One way to overcome this is to dip the treated part of the ear, not into talcum, but into dry mustard.

If your puppy is outdoors a great deal and giving you "ear trouble," kaolin can be a great nuisance because it washes off in the rain. In this case, use crude lanolin (wool fat) but it will have to be removed with rubbing alcohol.

Another method of "breaking" the tip of the ear is to use Antiphlogistine, a proprietary poultice. Dab a little onto the inside tip of the ear each day, gradually increasing the build-up. Antiphlogistine hardens and its weight acts to bend the tip of the ear forward. When the "Tulip ear" is set, the hardened poultice can be soaked off with warm water.

When you think the ears are right, leave them untreated for a day or two; then if they start going up again, get back to work. The crucial time in a Collie's life, as far as ear carriage is concerned, is during the period of teething, from four to nine months. You may have to persevere with ear training during this entire period, and possibly even afterward. Never give up. I have seen dogs whose ears were standing erect at the age of two years because nothing had been done, who, after some six months of really hard work, achieved the correct ear carriage which is such a large part of the whole, delightful expression of the Collie.

Selling Your Puppies

If your bitch is a good specimen you will have very little difficulty disposing of her puppies because her original breeder may be happy to help you; in fact, he may be willing to take all those puppies which you do not wish to keep. It is more for the novice who breeds an occasional litter that these paragraphs were written.

Remember first, that the sooner the puppies are sold, the less it costs you to keep them. This is not to suggest that you sell the puppies before they are properly weaned; but after they are about four weeks old, you can begin to explore the market. There are several advertising media, and it depends upon the quality of the puppies which you choose. Obviously, it would be a waste of money to advertise puppies that are only of "pet" quality in one of the specialist dog magazines. "Pet" quality puppies should be advertised in the pet columns of your daily or weekly newspaper. They can also be offered to local pet shop dealers.

Deciding what price to charge is always a problem, even for the experienced breeder, and although it is a good idea to add up just what it cost you to breed and rear the litter, you probably won't find the total very much help. What it will do is show you just how little you can hope to profit from any litter of puppies. However, if you use this method, don't forget to include the price of the stud fee, the cost of the extra food while your bitch was in whelp and while rearing her puppies, the cost of the veterinary advice, and the food during the weaning period. Add to this the average cost per week to maintain your bitch for one year, because you cannot hope to breed a Collie litter from the same bitch more than once a year. Total this sum and divide it by the number of puppies you have for sale. The result will come as a shock! You will probably find that the average price per puppy (and remember, these are just costs, no profit included) will be far higher than the price one can reasonably expect any person to pay for a pet puppy; so you will probably have to write the loss off to experience and interest.

It is far better to sell your puppy at eight weeks, taking a slight cut in the asking price, than to have him still running around four months later, when your loss will be even greater. I doubt that you will get a much higher price for a puppy four months old than you would one of eight weeks if he is only of "pet" quality. In fact, you may have to take less, and don't forget that in the interim your puppy has had to be immunized, an added expense. So do not hold out for an excessive price and find yourself saddled with half a dozen puppies, growing fast and eating "like horses". As puppies grow they become less attractive and cuddly, and their faults become even more noticeable. They are not so easy to sell.

Remember too, that you cannot expect to obtain the same price for your puppies that you paid for their mother who came from a kennel with a well-known name and reputation. Such reputations are built up over a long time at great expense, and a beginner with an unknown name can hardly expect similar financial rewards.

Advertising must be clear, concise and honest. It is no use to advertise "the perfect dog"; nobody will believe you, for such a dog does not exist. Describe him as accurately as possible, although, if you are describing just a pet puppy, it is not necessary to go into full details; no one replying to such an ad will expect a show puppy. However, if you have a puppy whom you think has a show future, and wish to advertise him in a specialist magazine give fuller details. Above all, state clearly what his breeding is, the price, and any information that may be of special interest; also state that complete details will be given on request.

Do try to answer all inquiries by return mail, or telephone. For the bigger kennel this is extremely difficult, because it will have a mass of correspondence, but prompt response does give the would-be purchaser the impression that you are interested in him and that he will receive courteous service. Look back to the time when you wrote your first letter, wanting to buy a puppy. Did you not wait expectantly for the arrival of the mailman, bearing the reply? I know I did.

When advertising a puppy for sale, remember to include in addition to the purchase price, the cost of air or rail travel. This expense should be paid by the purchaser.

The Novice Stud

Do not, please, imagine, because you purchased a male Collie puppy that turned into a good looking specimen able to win prizes in shows, that you have in your backyard a stud dog. First, it is only the novice breeder with perhaps one pet bitch who ever thinks of using the dog next door. Second, unless your dog has won a great many prizes, possibly even his championship title, he will never be in demand by any of the big breeders.

Not only this, but so many novices, be they owners of dogs or bitches, have the idea that putting their dog at stud, taking a nice fat fee, is just money for jam. Let me disillusion you at once.

Stud work can be one of the most time-consuming, time-wasting phases of the life of a kennel owner. Any successful stud dog must be trained to his job; otherwise he will waste time on every occasion that a bitch is brought to him – waste not only time, but energy, his and that of his owner.

Let us imagine that you own a young dog. Let us say that he is ten or eleven months old – the age at which a dog can first be used at stud – that he has done some winning, and that a friend of yours with one bitch has decided to mate her to him. All very fine, but wait! The bitch arrives when she is supposed to be "ready", somewhere, one would assume, around the 12th or 13th day; but as you read earlier, there is no certain rule about this. You introduce the dog to the bitch, and the dog looks at her and wonders, "Why has she bothered to come?" He has not the remotest idea, and she, if she is a maiden bitch, will have precious little idea why she is there.

The ideal arrangement for the first mating is with a bitch who has had two or three litters, and who knows what is expected of her. Such a bitch may well flirt with the dog and show him what to do. But even a flirtatious bitch may have no wiles for a youngster. He may be quite innocent, and you will probably turn red with embarrassment.

Very occasionally you may be lucky to find that your dog is a natural stud – that as soon as he is put in contact with a bitch in season, he knows what to do, gets on with his job, and turns it rapidly into a "fait accompli". But this I consider a rare dog. Collies are usually a little shy and backward at these moments, and actually need to be coached.

It will save time and energy if you teach your young stud from the word "go" that he can expect to have his bitches held for him; for there will come a day when an awkward bitch will turn and fly at the dog (possibly even fly at you) and you will have to hold her. If the dog has not been accustomed to this, he may well back off and reflect, "I want no part of that!"

Decide, before the first bitch arrives, where you wish the mating performed, and make this a permanent spot for future matings. Your dog will quickly come to associate this place with what he has to do. It may well be a corner of the yard, the garage, a shed; but whichever is chosen, it should have a non-slippery floor – concrete, not too smooth, is all right – but linoleum tile, or polished wood are useless.

Keep both animals on leashes. Let them rub noses but keep a careful watch on the bitch to make sure she does not wrinkle her nose preparatory to snapping at the dog, for a young dog snapped at during his first attempt may well be put off for a considerable time, if not for always. Another thing that is likely to put him off, and depress him, is if he fails to mate at this first service. He will be unhappy, go off his food and lose condition, and it is for this reason I stress that you obtain for him a bitch who has mated before and knows all the answers.

When you are quite sure that they are happy together, get an

Champion Kinmont Bobbie of Borco. Bobbie, owned by Coronation Kennels, is the sire of 11 champions.

assistant to hold the bitch by her head, while you encourage your dog to mount her. He may be backward and shy at this, but do not get impatient or lose your temper, because you may well discourage him forever. Encourage him every time he makes the slightest attempt to get onto the bitch. If he mounts her readily, place your hand under the bitch between her back legs, raising the vulva very slightly, so that you are able to feel the exact position of the penis, and so give the dog every possible assistance.

As soon as the dog penetrates the bitch, and starts to work, help him to retain his balance until he is, as we discussed earlier "tied". Give him a moment or two to relax and then help him to turn off the bitch, placing his forelegs on the ground first, and then turning him round with his back leg passing over the bitch's back, so that he is standing with his rear end toward hers. During all this time, once he has penetrated, keep congratulating him in a quiet voice, telling him what a clever boy he is, so that he will know he is pleasing you. and will have an even greater desire to do the job right next time.

When a stud is used for the very first time, it is possible that his semen may prove infertile, because if the sperm have remained there for some time, they may be dead. It is always advisable to give a second service if the dog has never been used before. The same is true if there has been a long lapse of time since the last service. Other than this, there is no reason why the dog should be asked to give more than one service. This first mating, if the bitch is willing and happy, should be perfectly adequate, and it is not fair of the bitch owner, particularly when going to a dog much in demand, to expect more than one satisfactory service.

The question of the stud fee will arise. I do not think it would be fair to take a fee at the time of mating, because your dog is not yet proved. Instead, arrange with the owner of the bitch that an agreed-upon sum of money will be paid when the puppies are born, or that you will take a puppy in lieu of the stud fee. This is entirely up to you. But after this first occasion a fee should be set for the dog, because the fee is payable for the service and not for the result. Before a dog is placed at public stud, he must be proved, that is to say he must have sired at least one live litter.

The stud dog must always be kept in fit condition. He cannot always be in full coat because this, of course, is seasonal, but he must never be allowed to get too fat, although he must be well-covered with flesh. He must be kept on an adequate diet, and during a peak breeding period, he should receive more protein than he would normally. Other than this, except for keeping him absolutely clean and free from parasites, there is nothing else to do for the stud dog.

Just one last word of caution – don't expect your stud to mate a bitch just after a long walk. If you know that a bitch is coming, shut him up for an hour or two before she is due to arrive, so that he may rest and be extra specially eager when they are introduced.

If your Collie is properly trained and has confidence in you he will look forward to traveling and visiting dog shows. Can anyone doubt that this blue merle is enjoying himself?

Experienced Collie owners judge their pets' state of health by their bright-eyed, shiny-coated, bushy-tailed appearance. The unknown owner of this lovely young dog in Sweden need have no concern.

XIV Your Dog's Health

When you have a dog in the house, it is just as necessary to be prepared for an accident to him, or for an illness – serious or minor – as it is with the human members of your family, so be sure that your dog's medicine cabinet stands ready for any emergency.

Here are a few things that it is wise to keep on hand:

Rectal Thermometer	Camphor
Sterile Cotton	Bicarbonate of soda
Bandages	Aspirin
Adhesive Tape	Ointment
Cotton-tip swabs	Antiseptic foot powder
Tweezers	Child's cough mixture
Eye Dropper	Mineral or olive oil
Curved Scissors	Potassium permanganate
Petroleum Jelly	Disinfectant
Alcohol	Eye drops
Peroxide	Ear drops

Temperature

The dog's normal temperature is 101 to 102.2° F and if it goes higher than that, say 103° F, and remains high for 24 hours, it should be considered a danger signal. Since a temperature rise is usually the first warning sign of an incipient illness, every owner should know how to take his dog's temperature.

Although there are special dog thermometers, an ordinary clinical thermometer is suitable, provided it is the blunt-end type, since the temperature must always be taken anally. Before inserting the thermometer check to see that the mercury is below 95°. Lightly grease or soap the thermometer and then insert it gently, very gently, into the rectum for about two-thirds of its length. Even if you are using a half-minute thermometer, leave it in place for a full minute, so you are sure to get a true reading. Never let go of the end of the thermometer.

If you find that there is a rise, put the dog away quietly for half an hour, and then take the temperature again, for as I said in the chapter on choosing a puppy, any dog may show a rise in temperature when he has just recently been exercised or excited. If at the end of an half hour's rest, his temperature is back to normal, I should not worry beyond the fact that I might well take it again and check the following day. If, however, at the end of the half hour the dog still has a rise of temperature of more than one degree, I would leave him for a further hour, and then retake the temperature. If it is still up, better seek professional advice, for a high temperature means that a dog is fighting infection and the sooner the disease is diagnosed and treated the better.

If on taking the temperature you find it seriously subnormal, (down to 100° F., or below) this is equally grave because a subnormal temperature can indicate many things, and the dog may well be on the point of collapse. In fact, a subnormal temperature would send me to a veterinarian with the greatest possible speed.

The young puppy, particularly one that has just started teething, may well run a slight temperature for no reason at all, but if it persists for more than 12 hours, I would still seek professional advice.

Inoculation

Puppies, like human babies, have not had time to build up an immunity to disease through exposure to it. A certain amount of protection is given a puppy by the antibodies in the colostrum which they first receive from their mother while nursing. This immunity lasts for several weeks after they have been weaned and serves to help protect them for that period of time.

Puppies can be given a long lasting immunity to Distemper by the time they are ten weeks old. Your veterinarian can also inoculate your puppy with antibodies which, while their effect is measured in days, will serve to protect him until he can receive his permanent inoculation. At the same time that he is giving the Distemper shots, your veterinarian will also immunize your puppy against Hepatitis and Leptospirosis. In the early stages, their symptoms are similar to those described for Distemper. An accurate diagnosis is best left to your veterinarian who is trained to differentiate.

Be safe – have your puppy immunized before any symptoms appear since the value of inoculation, once the disease has been contracted, is doubtful.

Distemper (Carre's Disease)

True Distemper, which is correctly called Carre's disease after the man who studied it, is seldom seen today thanks to our advanced methods of immunization. However, the word "Distemper" is frequently used in an over-all sense to indicate a dog with a generalized set of symptoms.

These symptoms are, in their early stages, very similar, and accurate diagnosis is almost impossible. They include a rise in temperature, mucous nose and/or eyes, loss of appetite, diarrhea, listlessness, frequent productive sneezing, vomiting, and a deep cough, low in the abdomen, as distinguished from a bronchial cough.

These symptoms are enough to make one suspect Distemper although, by themselves, they do not support diagnosis because as we have stated, several other serious diseases frequently show the same symptoms.

Additional indications of true Distemper are photophobia, or fear of light, a distinctive temperature curve, and conjunctivitis – an inflammation of the conjunctiva, the membranes lining the eyelids. The puppy will hide in dimly lit areas and when exposed to light, will squint and show his discomfort. Another distinctive symptom is the so-called diphasic, or saddle curve of temperature. From the normal of 101 to 102.2° F. the puppy's temperature will shoot up to as high as 105° F. on the fifth day after infection, followed by a drop to almost normal on the sixth. This is followed by a rise to 103° or 104° F. to remain there for the duration of the illness.

Frequently, pustules or sores will be seen on the stomach. The skin, when pinched, will retain the crease, returning back to normal slowly in contrast to a healthy skin which snaps back.

As these symptoms develop, keep the puppy warm, check its temperature daily, keeping a written record. This will help your veterinarian make a positive diagnosis if the symptoms do not subside. Part of a baby aspirin tablet can be given three or four times daily, and the puppy should be hand fed if necessary. Boil 4 ounces of milk and 4 ounces of water and allow the mixture to cool. Add 2 ounces of Karo Syrup, the yolk of an egg, a pinch of salt, and mix well. Feed it to the puppy freely. Should you have to resort to spoon feeding, pull out the lips at the side to form a pocket and pour in a spoonful at a time. Allow ample time for it to go down before giving another swallow. Make sure he gets a little nourishment often.

Simple diarrhea, as we said earlier, can be controlled by administering Kaopectate or milk of bismuth. For small puppies, give one tablespoon initially, followed by one teaspoon every three hours, or after every bowel movement. For larger dogs increase the dosage in proportion to the size.

If these symptoms persist, you must, of course call your veterinarian. However, do not become unduly discouraged. While Distemper, Leptospirosis, or Hepatitis when they do appear are extremely serious, antibiotics can help control any secondary infection and, with good nursing, there is a decent percentage of cures. Some, but by no means all, puppies are left with after-effects which may be scarcely noticeable in some and severe in others, but many do make a complete recovery. Should it turn out that it wasn't true Distemper after all, but one of the lesser puppy ailments, chances are good for a complete recovery.

Hardpad Disease

Some persons consider this to be a form of Distemper, possibly a sudden change in the virus of Carre. The symptoms of it are quite different but apparently the vaccines against Distemper are equally effective against hardpad. In many areas of America, hardpad is much more prevalent than Carre's Disease. The temperature does not rise as high, there is a slight amount of mucus from the nose and eyes, the stools are quite normal, where in the case of Carre's disease they may be bloody and evil smelling. The appetite is only slightly impaired. The chief characteristic is the hardening of the bottom surface of the foot pads and of the nose. Some dogs have flattened pads, others rounded. When walking over tile or concrete they sound as if the feet had marbles instead of toes.

In the great majority of cases the dog develops some symptom of brain inflammation: fits, twitches, and dies in a coma. There is no known cure but many dogs recover, some left with twitches which last the rest of their lives.

Tracheobronchitis

Usually called "Kennel Cough", this is one of the commonest ailments of puppies. It is characterized by a gagging cough during which the puppy seems to be attempting to clear his throat, or to throw up, but with little or no results. The cough is usually more severe during the night. Otherwise the puppy appears all right. Appetite and bowel movement are normal as is the temperature which should be between 101 and 102.2° F. The eyes and nose are clear. "Kennel Cough" is caused by a highly contagious virus which is particularly prevalent where puppies are kept under crowded conditions.

Fortunately, "Kennel Cough" is a self-limiting disease, that is, the dog will recover by itself without treatment, although the cough may persist as long as six weeks. Cough mixtures, obtainable at most pet counters, are often helpful; so are those prepared for children. For severe cases your veterinarian can prescribe Sulfa drugs, or one of the broad spectrum antibiotics such as chloromycetin, which will often relieve the coughing.

Leptospirosis (Infectious Jaundice)

There are two types of Leptospirosis – *Canicola* and *Icterohaemorrhagiae*. These diseases, to the inexperienced, are similar in appearance to Distemper. The incubation period is five to fifteen days. Weakness, loss of appetite, vomiting and a temperature of 103 to 105° are often symptoms of Leptospirosis. At the onset, the dog suffers a sharp drop in temperature, becomes quite depressed, breathes laboriously, and evinces a great thirst. This thirst is seldom present in attacks of Distemper. The dog also seems stiff and sore, particularly when rising from a sitting position.

Any of the above-mentioned symptoms are warnings to contact your veterinarian.

Leptospirosis is a disease spread by dog urine and by rats. It is often contacted from drinking water which has been contaminated by the urine of rats as well as from garbage dumps where rats have lived. This is why cleanliness and sanitation are so important in the care of your dog. Both forms can be contracted by human beings so it is a good idea to keep any affected dog in a pet hospital.

While there is some mortality with *Leptospirosis*, antibiotic treatment in the early stages, particularly, can reduce the danger considerably. Your veterinarian will know what to do.

Hepatitis (Inflammation of the Liver)

This is a virus disease that is also frequently mistaken for Distemper. It is particularly dangerous to puppies, which when infected may die, even before showing any noticeable symptoms. Usually a puppy who survives 24 to 48 hours after the onset has a fairly good chance of recovery. There is also very little likelihood of after-effects, such as nerve damage, from a Hepatitis attack.

One symptom frequently seen after a dog has had Hepatitis, is a blueing of one eye, or sometimes, both eyes. The cornea actually turns color until it looks like blue milk-glass. This is temporary and

This is Champion Glocamora Morning Mist. She is a top winning smooth Collie of all time, with a total of 102 Best of Variety awards. She won Best Smooth at the Collie Club of America Specialty Show, over 40 smooths in California in March, 1967, and has won from coast to coast. She is owned and shown by Isabel Chamberlin. Truly a remarkable record.

A wise precaution before taking your dog to a show or, for that matter, any place where dogs congregate, is to visit your vet for a booster inoculation.

passes away in a day or two, at which time the eye resumes its normal hue without further care or treatment. This condition may occasionally occur after vaccination. It is no cause for alarm as it is caused by the potency of the vaccine.

Fortunately, like Carré's disease, effective vaccination against this dread disease is also available. Your puppy should be protected against it as early as possible.

Rabies

Rabies is mentioned in this section because there are many misconceptions regarding it. Over the years, so much legend and mystery has grown up about it that the very name itself has become a "Fright word".

While rabies does at times cause fits, it is not one of the commonest causes. Fits are caused by an inflammation or damage of, or to, the brain, and this can be the result of a number of unrelated things.

Rabies is transmissible from animal to animal including bats and some cases from birds. It is not airborne, it is not caused by spontaneous generation nor can the dog carry it within itself until it is stimulated into activity by some circumstance.

The rabies virus itself must be introduced into the nervous tissue to cause an infection. Therefore, if your dog has *not* had any contact with a rabid animal. it cannot have rabies. This is particularly true in the case of puppies which playfully scratch or bite children and cause panic in the breast of the parent. To repeat, unless the puppy has been in contact with a rabid animal and been bitten, it cannot possibly have rabies. In fact, even if the rabies virus is spread on unbroken skin the infection will not develop.

When a rabid dog bites something, its teeth act as a hypodermic to drive the saliva deep into the tissues where infection takes place. Symptoms of the disease vary. The dog may or may not howl, and may or may not become ferocious. A rabid dog seems unable to drink water, although apparently anxious to do so. From this came the old name for the disease, "Hydrophobia", which means water-fearing. Actually, as we now know, they are not afraid of water, they are merely unable to swallow. Finally, rabies is much less prevalent than one would believe.

However, should your dog be bitten by a strange animal, or if you or anyone you know is bitten by a strange animal, if at all possible, confine the biting animal so it cannot escape or bite anyone else and immediately seek the advice of the health authorities. What we have said concerning rabies is not intended to make you contemptuous of, or to have you ignore, the possibilities of rabies infection. Rather, it is to put the picture in its proper perspective: that while rabies does exist, it is not prevalent except in certain areas where health authorities usually know of the danger, nor does every bite automatically mean rabies. All dog bites, of course, should be examined by a doctor, in the same way as any other wound would be looked after.

Your dog can be vaccinated so that he is not susceptible to rabies. This is the safest and wisest procedure to follow, particularly if you

This lovely dark red sable is Hercules of Heather, owned by Mr. and Mrs. John C. Parry. Male Collies mature late and at 5 years of age Hercules is in his prime. He has nine points towards his championship, including a Best of Variety.

are in a rabies area. Many areas, through care and precaution, have not known of rabies in years. For example, in New York City, according to an official of the health department, there has not been a case of rabies in 28 years. England, which has a quarantine on dogs entering that country, likewise is a rabies free area. The disease can be wiped out. One answer is proper vaccination.

Rabies Treatment*

First aid procedures are recommended in all rabies exposures, but particularly when a delay is anticipated before competent medical

* Dean, Donald J. *Local Wound Treatment of Animal Bites*. In "Proceedings, National Rabies Symposium," 1966.

treatment can be obtained. Fortunately many purported exposures to rabies are dubious or consist of bruises, abrasions, lacerations, and other minor wounds. Wounds should be encouraged to bleed freely whenever practical. The effectiveness of simple first aid procedures in guinea pigs suggests that similar procedures may be effective in man also. Marked sparing effect has resulted from the treatment of deep cutaneous wounds three hours after infection with approximately 1.000,000 LD_{50} of fixed rabies virus by scrubbing and flushing the wound with cotton pledgets impregnated with warm tap water, 20 percent soap solution, 1 percent aqueous benzalkonium chloride, or Ivory Soap and water, both with and without the addition of topically applied rabies antiserum. Despite severe challenge as manifested by 90 percent mortality in the control animals, not more than two animals in each treated group died of rabies; these differences between controls and treated groups are hightly significant statistically. Trappers, laboratory workers, and others in high risk occupations should, in addition to being vaccinated prior to exposure, have ready access to first aid supplies including 1 percent aqueous Zephiran and/or 20 percent soft soap solution. Wherever practical, hyperimmune serum or its gamma globulin preparation should be available for possible topical application.

Treatment by the physician should include thorough cleansing and debridement followed by thorough swabbing and irrigation of the wound with copious amounts of a 1 percent aqueous solution of benzalkonium chloride (Zephiran) or 20 percent soft soap solution. Such treatment has been shown to be effective by many workers. However, Zephiran should be used judiciously on or near delicate tissues. Other substances should not be used without adequate prior testing. Quaternary ammonia compounds, for example, are not equally effective in preventing rabies. Adequate cleansing with benzalkonium chloride or soap is believed to be at least as effective and probably more so than fuming nitric acid in wounds that permit its application. Immediate suturing of the wound is not generally advised since it may contribute to the development of rabies. Antibiotics presently available do not affect rabies virus but may be helpful in preventing bacterial infection.

Convulsions or Fits

These are names for the same thing. I differentiate them here by describing the minor attacks of puppies as fits and the more serious ones that victimize all dogs – grownups as well as puppies – as convulsions.

Puppy fits are usually caused by one of three things – worms, lumpy food, or teething. If caused by worms, fits are inexcusable, because if a puppy is so infested with worms that fits result, the condition should never have been allowed to reach this stage. If it has, then professional help is the only solution because you could easily kill a puppy so badly infested if you tried to treat it yourself.

Fits caused by teething are not uncommon in Collies because, quite often, Collie puppies have difficulty cutting their teeth – the gums become sore and swollen; it is in such cases that teething fits occur. Fits can also be caused by lumps of very coarse food in the stomach.

A puppy suffering from these minor fits should be kept queitly isolated in a cool semi-dark room until such time as you are able to get a veterinarian. You can give the pup a mild sedative to keep him quiet until the vet arrives. Any dog having a fit should always be kept isolated from other dogs or puppies because the natural tendency of a pack is to attack the weaker member. If your Collie should have a fit in the presence of other dogs, it might be seriously injured before you could separate it from its companions.

Convulsions are more serious. Before the development of vaccinations against the more common diseases of what is called the Distemper Complex, convulsive attacks were much more common than they are today. They usually indicate brain inflammation, often as an end result of some virus disease. The ingestion of certain poisons, injuries to the brain, even the toxins exuded by certain worms may cause them.

It is difficult even for an expert to diagnose their basic cause. One general rule of thumb is to note whether the dog maintains consciousness and awareness of his surroundings during the attack. Should he pass out, lose consciousness or awareness, the probable cause is a brain injury, most likely viral in origin.

Very often such convulsions herald an unfavorable turn. A dog may apparently be recovering from a viral disease such as hardpad, and then, just about the time you expect him to improve rapidly, convulsions set in. The dog may froth at the mouth and become rigid. He may have what are sometimes called "chewing gum fits" in which he chomps his jaws repeatedly, salivating copiously. He may also defecate or urinate. Many die, but some recover. As he recovers from such an attack, the dog is usually dizzy. Do not make the common mistake of confusing it with rabies. A rabid dog never recovers.

Should he retain consciousness but show an inability to control his actions – that is jerking, twitching, barking, collapsing, while making an effort to retain his balance and control – it is quite possible that the convulsion is not viral-induced but the result of a toxin in his system. This may be something he has ingested or be from some other cause which can be successfully treated.

Do not try to pick up a dog having a convulsion. Have faith that he will soon be over it. When he is, clean him up, and take him to the veterinarian where you can leave him for diagnosis and treatment. If you have observed anything that may have caused the convulsion, such as symptoms of a disease or injury from a fall or a blow from which he has apparently recovered, be sure to tell this to your vet. Your dog may recover completely or he may be left with a twitch in some group of muscles, depending upon what areas of the brain are damaged. This twitch may remain with him for life; it may get better or it may become more marked. Unfortunately, there is no way of predicting.

Tonsillitis

Dogs, like humans, have tonsils that may become infected and inflamed causing sore throat and coughing. At times this infection may be the result of, or a secondary condition of, another disease. Large-headed dogs, like English Bulldogs and Boston Terriers, frequently have chronic tonsillitis due to the formation of their throats.

The prompt administration of antibiotics is the key to the successful treatment of tonsillitis.

Advanced chronic tonsillitis may make it necessary to remove the tonsils surgically. Your veterinarian is the best judge of what should be done. A soft tasty diet is advisable during the treatment of tonsillitis in order to relieve any difficulty in swallowing.

Colds

Colds as we know them in humans are not found in dogs. However, there are many ailments, most of them minor in nature, which have a somewhat similar appearance. Some fever, listlessness, diarrhea slight runniness of the nose and/or eyes, and a general lethargy are the symptoms. Keep the dog warm and feed a soft diet. Diarrhea should be treated as given below. Feed a soft, bland diet, easily digested, until the symptoms have passed. Many veterinarians recommend feeding, when a dog is not well, equal amounts of chopped meat and rice mixed together with the addition of 10 % canned stewed tomatoes. This should be fed as the sole diet until the dog has returned to normal.

Should the symptoms persist for several days without lessening, it is best to seek professional help.

Diarrhea

Diarrhea, frequently accompanied by vomiting, is quite common in young puppies. Your first contact with it may be as you drive your puppy home from where it was purchased. Due to the excitement and the motion of the car, it is not unusual for puppies to throw up and the upset stomach may cause diarrhea. This is why many puppy purveyors recommend a bland, easily digested diet such as that recommended for *Colds*, for the first few days a puppy is in a new home.

Frequently, sudden, drastic changes in diet may upset a dog's stomach and cause diarrhea.

A puppy's habit of picking up foreign matter, such as bits of plastic, hair, fur, matchsticks, cigarette butts, what-have-you, which he may find lying about or behind the furniture will frequently cause an upset stomach. For years I could not understand why some puppy owners insisted that their dogs did not eat any foreign objects even when they were shown, by microscopic examination of the stool, that their puppy had ingested such matter. Then I realized that this was a paradoxical question. If the owner actually saw the puppy eating the wrong things, he would stop the practice. Obviously, the puppy was doing it at times, or in places of which the owner was not aware.

Diarrhea, unless it is a symptom of some disease, is not usually difficult to cure. The aforementioned bland diet and limiting the amount of water are usually sufficient. A teaspoon to several tablespoons of either milk of bismuth or Kaopectate given at three to four hour intervals for a few days will also help bind the dog. The amount to be given varies according to the weight of the dog. Diarrhea is frequently accompanied by a mucousy or slimy appearance of the bowel movement and after several loose movements, blood may be seen in the stool. This is not necessarily a symptom of a serious disease but may indicate an infection of Coccidiosis. However, diarrhea in itself is debilitating and should not be allowed to persist. If the dog seems lively, eyes clear and bright, no mucus at the nose, and with a normal appetite, treat as we have described. Should any other symptoms appear, or if the diarrhea does not respond to treatment within a few days, it is best to seek professional help.

Feeding cow's milk is frequently cited as a cause for diarrhea in puppies. The cause is probably not only just the milk itself but also the change of diet when giving milk to a puppy who is not accustomed to it or in giving skimmed milk after a puppy has been having the high fat milk from its mother.

When introducing milk into a new puppy's diet, it is best to boil the milk and than add it in small amounts, gradually increasing the amounts of the new item to the accustomed diet. Light cream or evaporated milk is preferable to ordinary milk. This is why it is important when purchasing a dog to ask the previous owner what he has been feeding, and continue the same diet until the dog is adjusted.

Lady Popinjay of Heather is bred and owned by Mr. and Mrs. John C. Parry. She is 3 years old, has just started showing, and already has three points. In Baltimore County Kennel Show in 1966 Lady took Best of Opposite Sex.

TOM CARAVAGLIA

Bad Breath

Smelly breath is sometimes a symptom of disease, but it is usually attributed to bad diet – to too much meat, to bad teeth or to tartar on the teeth. This last means that your dog's teeth should be cleaned – either scaled by a veterinarian, or scrubbed with hydrogen peroxide solution or with toothbrush and ordinary toothpaste.

Give the dog some hard dog biscuits every day or some soft rib bones and he will scale the tartar from his teeth himself. Occasionally bad breath is attributable to a stomach disorder; for this your vet's advice should be sought if a dose of bicarbonate of soda doesn't do the trick. A diet too rich in meat may also cause bad breath. Substitute more vegetables and cereal.

Anal Glands

At each side of the anus the dog has small organs, known as the anal glands. Many Collies go through life without these glands giving them any trouble at all; occasionally, they may have to be cleared by squeezing. The indications are when the dog is constantly sitting down and dragging his rear along the ground, or when having a bowel movement, he expresses pain by crying although the feces are soft. The expressing of these glands is fairly simple, but it is something you must be shown how to do, so if you suspect that your dog is afflicted, take him to the veterinarian, who will show you how. But there is a certain knack to it, and I for one, after many years, have never gotten this knack – I find I simply cannot do the job.

INTERNAL AND EXTERNAL PARASITES

Worms

Worms are prevalent among dogs, particularly when puppies. Some estimates of the incidence of worm infestation run as high as 90 % at some time in a dog's life. That is, 90 % of all the dogs you see or own are likely to have worms at one time or another. This is not as serious as it may sound at first, as many dogs seem to live with the worms, suffering little, if any, ill effects. However, a dog should never be allowed to harbor worms, particularly when a veterinarian has the means for diagnosing their presence, differentiating between the species, and medicating your dog safely and simply.

In order to make an accurate diagnosis, it is usually necessary to take a stool specimen to your veterinarian. Only a small amount is required, approximately a thimbleful and this can be taken in a small glass jar labelled with your name and the name of your dog. The veterinarian has facilities to separate the eggs from the bowel evacuation and to make a microscopic examination.

General symptoms indicating the presence of worms follow. When infested with Roundworms, a puppy's stomach will bloat up and seem out of all proportion. Some types of worms cause extreme emaciation. The dog has a normal appetite but does not seem to put on weight. A cough which lasts for only a few days may be due to the presence of worm larvae in the esophagus. Watery eyes and/or runny nose are also symptoms.

Heavy mucus of the nose and/or eyes, however, usually indicates a more serious ailment requiring immediate veterinary attention. Look at the dog's gums: they should be pink. If they are gray the pup may be anemic from hookworm infestation. Frequently a dog will sit on his haunches and drag his rear end along the ground. This is commonly mistaken as a symptom of worms. It is usually due, as I said, to impacted anal glands.

Whipworms. These are seldom if ever encountered in very young puppies.

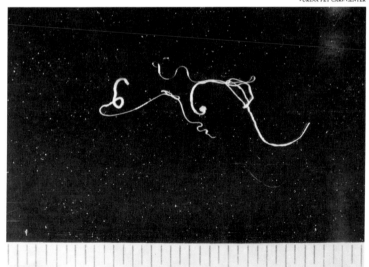

How Dogs Contract Worms

Most worms come from eggs which are passed in the stool. When a dog noses where others have defecated, he picks the eggs up on his nose, licks it, swallows them, and becomes infected. Sometimes an owner will carry worm eggs home on his shoes. A nursing puppy may be infected by its mother or from a stool clinging to her feet. Hookworms can even enter through the skin of a dog's body or stomach, particularly when the dog is kept in filthy surroundings. Tape worms are carried by fleas which serve as an intermediate host. Another form is contracted by eating rabbits.

Therefore, we see the importance of keeping our pets clean and away from contact with other dogs which may be carriers; we must also make sure that all fleas are destroyed as rapidly as possible.

Whipworms

Whipworms are seldom if ever encountered in very young puppies. They are primarily a disease of dogs three months of age or older. It is much commoner in the south and other warmer areas. This is a worm which is very seldom seen in the stool of the dog. Whipworm eggs incubate in the soil for about six weeks. This incubation takes place only during warm weather; however, the eggs are highly resistant to freezing and may last for years until the warmth enables them to maturate. The worm develops within the egg and lies dormant until swallowed by some animal. The digestive juices dissolve the coating of the egg, liberating the parasite which then attaches itself to the intestine of the dog.

Not as common as the Roundworm, Hookworm or Tapeworm, the Whipworm too can be completely eliminated by proper medication.

Roundworms

Roundworms are more dangerous to the puppy than to the older dog who seems to develop a kind of resistance or immunity to them. But, in puppies they have been known to cause death. The adult worms are long and spaghetti-like in appearance and when expelled by the dog, either by vomiting or in the stool, they coil themselves into a characteristic watch-spring shape, hence the name, "Roundworm".

Roundworm larvae can live in the bloodstream of a pregnant bitch

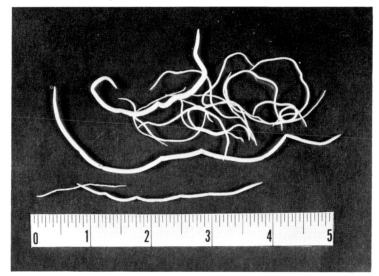

Roundworms. These are the commonest type of worms found in puppies, and are frequently expelled by the dog, either by vomiting or in the stool. Usually they coil themselves into a characteristic watchspring shape; hence the name "Roundworm".

and be passed on to the puppy. This is why it is important to worm a pregnant bitch in the early stages of her gestation, and to prevent her from picking up worm eggs during pregnancy. However, if this is neglected, worm the puppies when they are two or three weeks old, and again when they are four or five weeks old. A new medication based on a drug called piperazine can be given to puppies or adults either directly in a capsule or pill, or as a powder, in the food or drink. This treatment should be repeated in 12 to 13 days in order to break the life cycle of the worm. This is because the drug expels the adult worm but leaves the larvae circulating in the blood. The trick is to allow the larvae to get from the blood to the intestine and then eliminate the baby worms before they, in their turn, have had time to mature enough to lay eggs.

Hookworms

This is a tiny parasite, as thin as a thread and only half an inch long,

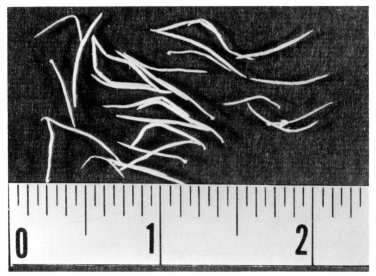

Hookworms. This is a tiny parasite as thin as a thread and only half-an-inch long. Notice the hook-life feature on one end of the worm.

Tapeworms. Note the segments! These frequently drop off and are passed out with the bowel movement.

in contrast to the Roundworm which can be one-sixteenth of an inch thick and three to four inches long. Hookworms look like white threads in the dog's stool. Each worm can suck blood at the approximate rate of a thimbleful a week. Heavy infestation can, and frequently does, cause death to puppies. A dog infected with Hookworm frequently has very pale membranes, so pull down the lower eyelid and examine the membrane. The gums may also be much lighter in color than normal. This is due to the functional anemia caused by the worms sucking his blood. They also give off a toxin which can produce fits. These are transitory and, provided the condition (i.e., the Hookworm) is cleared up in time, no permanent damage will result. (See section on *Convulsions*). Because of the anemia caused by the worms, it is wise to add a little iron to the diet to counteract any deficiency. Hookworm, too, can be eliminated either by a special worm capsule or by an injection.

Tapeworms

Tapeworms are long flat worms composed of many segments, like sausages linked together and then flattened out. The rear segments which carry the eggs frequently drop off and are passed out with the bowel movement. These segments can then be seen; they look like flattened brown or pink grains of rice in the hair around the anus or in the stools. It is commonly believed that Tapeworms cause an enormous increase in appetite, but actually, the reverse is true. The presence of Tapeworms depresses the appetite, frequently causes an unthrifty appearance and, at times, coughing.

Because of the way they are passed, Tapeworm eggs are frequently not seen by the veterinarian when he examines the stool of the dog to determine the presence of parasites. So it is up to the dog owner to keep a sharp eye on his dog to detect the presence of these parasites when they are passed, at which time they are clearly visible.

One form of Tapeworm requires an intermediate host – the flea. The flea larva feeds on dog stools with tapeworm segments in it, matures and lives on the dog, the dog eats the flea and the whole cycle begins again. The flea bite itself does not cause the eggs to pass from flea to dog. The easiest and most practical way to prevent your dog from becoming infected is to keep him free of fleas.

The rabbit-host Tapeworm eggs are usually found in a fecal examination. The rabbit must have eaten vegetation to which Tapeworm eggs were clinging. The egg becomes a larva which forms a cyst in the rabbit's liver or muscles and when the dog eats the rabbit, his digestive juices dissolve the cysts, liberating the Tapeworm head. This attaches itself to the intestine and segments grow from it, so many that the whole worm may be 18 inches long. Tapeworm infestation is a little more difficult to treat than the other types of worms, but with today's modern medicines, there is no reason for your dog to suffer from Tapeworm.

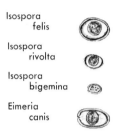

Isospora
    felis

Isospora
    rivolta

Isospora
    bigemina

Eimeria
    canis

The eggs of four different types of Coccidia which can infect dogs. These eggs are passed by the infected dog, and when encountered by another can start a new cycle of infection.

Coccidiosis

Very few if any dogs go through life without having a "siege" with a disease caused by a microscopic organism, coccidium. The disease is called coccidiosis (cock-sid-e-osis). Three principal forms affect dogs. The younger the dog, the more serious are the effects. Puppies at weaning time, when infected, show a loss of appetite, loose stools which are often bloody, and loss of weight.

The disease cannot, as yet, be cured but its effects can be greatly lessened by the use of drugs your veterinarian can supply or for which he will write a prescription. The worst cases are those of puppies who have been taken from their mother with her high-fat milk, and placed on a diet of skim milk. Such puppies often die. The diet which, besides drugs, helps most with recovery consists of light cream instead of skim milk, and plenty of Vitamin A which can be supplied by giving one drop of percomorph oil with each meal.

The duration of the symptoms is about three weeks. For the first and third weeks they are mild but during the middle week, they can be alarming. Once recovered, the dog is immune to further attacks although he will, in common with most dogs, be a life-long carrier.

If you buy a puppy and it develops watery stools, your veterinarian can learn the cause. If it is coccidiosis, the disease is probably at its worst and will soon start to subside. If you sell a puppy and a buyer complains about loose stools after having the dog a week or so, you may be able to explain that it is perhaps all to the good to get the trouble over with now. If the pup becomes infected when larger, there will be much more to clean up.

Fleas, Ticks and Lice

At one time, it was believed that fleas and other parasites were unavoidable adjuncts to keeping a dog. Today we know better. There are many powders, sprays, dips, collars, and internal medications that can eliminate these annoying and harmful pests. There is no excuse for having a parasite-ridden dog.

However, in order to eliminate these parasites completely we should know a little about them how to recognize them, how they infect a dog, and their life cycle so that we can bring them to an end.

Ctenocephalides canis

CHET PLEGGE, D.V.M.

Flea circuses are fun to watch, but fleas on your dog are not. Today, we can and should eliminate this pest.

Fleas

Fleas are probably the most common parasite. There used to be an expression, "As common as fleas on the belly of a hound dog".

This need not and should not be true today.

Fleas are tiny black insects that infest the hairy coat of your pet. Hidden by the hair, they are sometimes not seen. However, if you part the hair quickly you may see them scurrying for cover. They are difficult to catch, hard-shelled, and can make tremendous leaps. Another indication of their presence are sores on the less hairy section of the abdomen. These look, for all the world, like mosquite bites on a human being. Flea droppings resemble black specks of dirt.

Both male and female fleas infest the dog, the female laying eggs that drop off to the floor or ground. These eggs hatch, complete their development, and then the young flea crawls up any object eight to twelve inches from the ground and lies in wait for a passing animal, onto which it leaps. At this stage, fleas have been known to leap on humans. While it may be a blow to our vanity, the flea really prefers the dog, and although fleas have been known to bite humans, they leave as soon as possible to take up their preferred abode on man's canine or feline companions.

Many owners are astonished when they return from a vacation to a house which has been closed for weeks to find it infested with fleas. As you can see by the foregoing description of the cycle, this is the batch from the eggs laid prior to the dog's departure. The fleas are waiting for hosts.

Consequently, in order to deflea a dog properly and keep him free of the pests, it is not only necessary to use a flea killer on the animal but also on his surroundings. There are many good commercially prepared flea killers on the market which can be used to spray the interior of a house; concentrate particularly on the dog's bed and other resting places, after you have disinfected the dog. Since fleas crawl all over the dog, for ordinary preventive measures it is necessary merely to spray or dust one or two areas. As the fleas travel about they encounter the poison and are destroyed.

The latest and simplest method of flea control is by the use of a drug called Vapona. This can be purchased incorporated in a resin strip about ten inches long. It can be hung close to the dog. Its fumes, completely unobjectionable, will kill all the fleas on the dog and in his bed or environment.

The most effective flea control consists of using the 90 Day™ dog collar. When worn around the dog's neck, the collar eliminates fleas anywhere on your pet for three full months. It also helps in the control of ticks.

Lice

There are several types of lice classified into sucking lice which remain in one spot, and biting lice which travel slowly about the dog. Unlike fleas, lice spend their entire life cycle on a dog. The eggs which are fastened to the hairs can be seen on close examination, looking like translucent, tiny, white globules. These are called nits. Infection is by direct contact. Insecticides are available. Follow the directions on the package.

Ticks

At one time ticks were confined primarily to southern areas. However, as the world weather seems to have grown warmer, with milder winters, the tick has advanced, and is continuing to advance, northward, until it has become a problem in areas as far north as New York State, and even in Canada.

The two commonest types are the Brown Tick and the American Dog Tick. The American Dog Tick primarily is a parasite of the countryside while the Brown Tick is found inside buildings. Only the female is parasitic. The male – a small flat creature – is usually found under the engorged body of the female. The female is also a small flat creature until she attaches herself to your pet, sinking her mouth parts into the skin. There she remains sucking blood until she swells up to the size of a small grape. You may feel one of these on your dog while you are petting or stroking it. Touch the tick with an alcohol-dipped swab, and then use a tweezer to pull it off. Be careful to grip the tick as close to the head as possible so that you do not break off the mouth parts. Don't be alarmed if a tiny bit of skin comes away with it; this is better than leaving the mouthpart in the skin where it can cause infection. Peroxide makes a good antiseptic.

The engorged female tick will drop off the dog and crawl into a protected area where she can lay as many as 6000 eggs. Her life cycle completed she will die but the eggs, after completing their cycle, will produce young which, like fleas, crawl up about a foot onto plants and wait along a path for an animal host to which they can attach themselves. Ticks pass several stages of development, needing blood to develop. The last stage is the huge beanshaped creature.

The Brown Dog Tick which seems to prefer, as we mentioned

above, buildings, frequently infests houses. They can be brought in on house plants. Fortunately, the tick will not live on humans, preferring dog hosts. However, once they have become established in a building it may be necessary to engage the services of a professional exterminator to eliminate them.

There are powders, sprays, and dips available for treating ticks as well as the other parasites. However, because of the greater resistance of ticks to insecticides, be sure that the powder you are using specifies ticks on the label. Ordinary flea care products are usually not strong enough to kill ticks.

Insecticidal sprays intended for purposes other than pets should never be used on a dog. Such things as agricultural sprays or large-animal sprays may contain products which are toxic to pets.

In some countries there is a type of tick which causes paralysis, so if you know that this tick – an absolute killer – is prevalent in your area never, for one moment, leave a suspected one on your dog. Nor should you try to get rid of it yourself; take your dog to the veterinarian.

Eczema

Eczema is a disease which can appear in two forms – moist or dry. It is non-contagious, and the moist is frequently a seasonal complaint. It can even appear overnight with no apparent reason for its occurrence. It may easily be caused by irritation from a parasite; and infection starts from scratches; it is more usual during hot weather. It can occur anywhere on the body, and when it does, the whole of that area will become raw, red, and devoid of hair, and it will take a considerable time to clear up. The area around it should have the hair cut short; be careful when doing this because the affected area is always extremely sensitive. Moist eczema should not be confused with mange in either of its forms: it frequently responds to treatment with calamine lotion. However, when you meet it for the first time, it might be wise to take veterinary advice.

Dry eczema looks quite different – flaky, more like dandruff. It too is non-contagious; but as it is by no means easy to tell from mange, it is always wise to let your veterinarian see the animal, because while dry Eczema is relatively simple to deal with, mange is not, and a diagnosis can usually be made only by scraping a bit of skin and examining it under a microscope.

This is the mite *Demodex folliculorum,* the causative agent of Demodex or Demodectic Mange.

Mange

Mange exists in two different forms – sarcoptic and demodectic. Both are caused by parasites, so tiny that they can only be seen under the microscope. Sarcoptic mange is caused by a mite known as the *Sarcoptes scabei* var. *canis* which digs into the skin; **Demodectic mange** by *Demodex folliculorum.* This latter mite causes skin damage and the skin is then invaded by various bacteria which cause the boils and pus associated with demodectic mange. The disease starts innocently enough, usually with a small round or oval shaped baldish area on the cheeks or the front or sides of the legs where the hair is short. From these areas, it spreads out until it can cover the entire body. It causes itching, and by scratching, the dog spreads the mites to other areas. This type of mange is serious indeed; it may cause death from exhaustion, or toxemia.

Sarcoptic mange: This should be treated at once since secondary bacterial infections may occur. These are greatly to be dreaded as they may take three months or more to cure, and treatment involves

Sarcoptes scabiei – var. *canis.* **This is the Sarcoptic Mange mite, causative** organism of the disease known as Sarcoptic or Red Mange.

using medicated baths and lotions. Red, angry patches with crusts on them are found on the inner sides of the flanks, the belly and the legs. In warm weather the skin exudes a stale, mouse-like smell. The irritation is considerable. At one time it was believed that the infection was transmissible to human beings as Scabies. The Sarcoptic mange mite (*Sarcoptes scabei* var. *canis*) is not the same as the mite causing Scabies in humans (*Sarcoptes scabei*) and it cannot reproduce on a human being. A case of Sarcoptic mange should be placed under professional care at once.

Ringworm

Ringworm is not a worm but a fungus. It is characterized by ring-shaped discolored patches on the skin. Since it affects human beings as well as animals, always be extremely cautious when treating an infected dog. Let the veterinarian diagnose and prescribe. Let me say it now, if I haven't already, that in all skin ailments the symptoms are superficially the same and, since some of them are much more dangerous than others, professional treatment is always the wiser course.

Nursing the Ailing Dog

Because of a Collie's strong attachment to one particular person, he nearly always gets well quicker if nursed at home where he knows the people and his surroundings than if he is hospitalized. It is up to you to do your very best for your dog, if you are unfortunate enough to have one that requires nursing.

First and foremost, carry out the instructions of your veterinarian to the letter, following doctor's orders exactly as if you were nursing a human being.

The essentials you must provide include an adequate, comfortable bed – his own if possible, because he will naturally prefer to have something to which he is accustomed. He must have quiet and warmth and, of course, the diet prescribed by your veterinarian. Your love will prove a big factor in his recovery, and I must again remind you of the tremendous instinct a Collie has for sensing your thoughts. If you have any idea in your mind that he will not recover, then assuredly he will not. If you are bright and cheerful, you are much more likely to have a fine, healthy dog again.

Try not to keep a sick dog on the floor, because even the best built houses do have drafts low down, and, above all, an invalid must be kept out of them. If it is absolutely necessary, make sure that the area is completely draft proof. If your dog cannot use his usual bed, make him a bed on a pile of sacks and newspapers and put a screen around them.

Do not fuss over a sick dog. Do not keep running back to him every five or ten minutes to see if he is all right. Keep him in a room close to you or in a shed just outside the door where he is readily available and where, if anything happens unexpectedly, you can hear him, and do give him time, plenty of time, to sleep and rest quietly. This is what he most needs, and what will make the greatest contribution to his recovery.

One of the biggest difficulties in nursing a sick dog is to keep him clean, for as is probable, if he is a well housetrained dog, he will not want to make messes on the floor or in his bed. If his illness is slight, he can be taken outside to relieve himself; if not, it is up to you to keep him spotlessly clean, because it will add greatly to his discomfort when he relieves himself in or around his bed if he is left lying in the mess. Even if he has gone outdoors, check on his return to make quite sure that he is perfectly clean, so that there is no risk of carrying dirt back into his bed.

If your dog is paralyzed or so weak that he cannot move around, it will be up to you to keep turning him at regular intervals, so that he does not become stiff and uncomfortable from always lying on the same spot. Furthermore, you will risk his contracting pneumonia, and he will almost certainly break out in bedsores from lying too long in the same position, so it is up to you to see that the dog is turned from time to time, but not so often that his rest is disturbed,

As with a sick human, the vitality of a sick dog is at its lowest ebb during the night, and very often it becomes necessary to keep him warmer during these hours. This may be done with hot water bottles (but remember they must always be kept covered) or, easier for you and the dog, by an infra-red lamp. This must be used only after consultation with the veterinarian because of the possibility of dehydration, but, sensibly used, such a lamp is almost always of benefit.

In practically every case, unless decreed otherwise by the vet, the sick dog should always have a good supply of *fresh* drinking water. Here I stress the word *fresh*, for, especially if an infra-red lamp is in use, water quickly becomes lukewarm and uninviting, so change it frequently.

If a sick dog refuses food, it is not usually anything to worry about, for a dog can survive with no ill-effects far longer than can a human being without eating. A dog may be coaxed, but never forced to eat. He has probably decided for himself that a few days starvation will be good for him, so never try force-feeding until such measures are advised by the vet.

With a long-coated breed such as ours, the problem of grooming a sick dog is always a difficult one. If he is ill for just a few days, no grooming will be necessary, but if he is sick for a long period then, for his own comfort, some tidying up must be undertaken daily. The eyes should be bathed, daily at least, with warm water, and if they are discharging mucus, the lids should be kept lightly smeared with a little olive oil. Likewise, any nasal discharge could be cleansed several times a day with a wad of cotton dipped in warm water, and then the nostrils and nose should be wiped with olive oil.

In hot weather, and in a hot climate, the problem of flies worrying the patient is always tricky. His head should be wiped off daily, and great care taken to see that no spilt food is left adhering to the dog, nor dirty dishes left in his box.

His tail and feathering should also have regular attention, and it is possible to use a little disinfectant or some kind of fly repellant in the wash water on all parts of his body except around the eyes.

If your veterinarian wants a temperature chart kept, do remember, as has already been stressed, to take the animal's temperature before he can become in any way excited. Never forget to record the temperature, for it is all too easy to think you will remember and then find that you have no idea what the last reading was.

If medication is ordered be quite certain that it is given with absolute regularity, and also be sure that the dog, if not a really sick one, gets no chance to "run rings around you". He must be made to take his medicine; in this you must be very firm. A drug which has to be given "three times a day" means at eight hour intervals, not three times between 10 a.m. and 10 p.m., for instance. With many new drugs their value depends upon a constant level of that drug being in the patient's blood, so remember, every four hours means just what it says, as does any other kind of direction. It is not fair to your dog, or to your vet, not to carry out, absolutely to the letter, any instructions you are given.

This is not a safe way to administer liquid, as there is a possibility of its running down his windpipe. It is better to hold the dog's mouth closed, pull out the lips at the side of the mouth to form a pocket, and pour the liquid into this in small amounts.

If your vet has reason to doubt your reliability, then he has every right to hospitalize your dog; with a Collie, this can be serious, for your Collie would very much rather be with you. He is much more likely to make a rapid recovery if not separated from the person he loves. Since his life may well depend on you, your sacrifice is nothing compared to his life and love.

Administering Liquids

If it becomes necessary to administer liquids to your dog, it is best to know how to go about it. Opening the dog's mouth wide and pouring liquid down may result in its entering the windpipe and strangling the dog.

Hold the dog's mouth closed and his head up. With the other hand, pull out the lips at the side of the mouth to form a pocket. Pour liquid in small amounts into this pocket, a little at a time, waiting between swallows. Should the dog be strong and active, it helps to have an assistant pour the liquid while you hold the dog's head up and lips out.

Frequently a dog can be induced to take liquids on his own volition by sweetening them with Karo or honey. If he is reluctant at first, dip your finger in the mixture and dab a little on his nose. He will lick this off and get the taste and this may save you the trouble of hand feeding.

Administering Pills

Place the palm of your hand flat on the dog's skull. If you are using your right hand, your thumb should be on the left side of the dog's head pressing against the angle where the jaws meet, with your thumb and index finger at the angle on the right. Press the lips firmly against the teeth at the point where the upper and lower jaws meet and the pressure will cause the dog to open its mouth. The pill should be held ready in the other hand and popped into the dog's mouth as far back as it can go. If the dog is still a puppy, use the index finger as a pusher and poke the pill all the way down. You will feel a tightness in the throat. Make sure the pill is past this point or the dog will spit it back up. Don't be afraid of making the dog vomit, by pushing too far back; it just doesn't happen. If your dog is a large one, use your middle and index fingers as pushers. Do not try to use your thumb and index fingers to push down a pill since they cannot be inserted far enough into the dog's throat.

Should a dog's appetite be normal, and the pill not too large, you can usually induce him to swallow it by hiding it in a little chunk of raw meat and rolling the meat in salt. As dogs normally do not chew any more than necessary, giving a small chunk usually results in his swallowing it whole.

To administer pills, press the lips firmly against the teeth at the point where the upper and lower jaws meet. The pressure will cause the dog to open its mouth.

Collies are gentle dogs and two will live together in harmony.

XV First Aid

The well-informed pet owner should familiarize himself with this section of the book so that he will know what to do in the event of an emergency. This is not to say that accidents happen frequently to dogs; they do not. The average city dog may go through life without ever having a call of an emergency nature.

First aid is emergency treatment. It is intended to care for or relieve the pain problem of the animal until professional help can be obtained. Accidents frequently happen at times or at places when a veterinarian is not available. So, in the unlikely event that something should happen, be prepared.

Restraint

A dog suffering, in pain, and bewildered because of the suddenness and severity of an accident may on occasion revert to a semi-wild state. This is particularly true if the dog you are caring for does not know you, but it may happen with your own beloved pet. Approach the dog gently, speaking soothingly and watching his eyes and head for any sign of response. Should he snarl, bare his teeth or attempt to bite, it is best to improvise a muzzle, This can be a strip of cloth about two inches wide and approximately three feet long. A loop is formed in the center, and slipped over his jaws, then drawn tight with the knot under his chin. The loose ends are drawn back around his head and tied in a bow-knot behind the ears. This will prevent him from biting. Now attempt to make him lie down by holding the nape of his neck and pulling his hind legs out from under him.

For large dogs it may be necessary to use a lasso. The noose is thrown over the dog's head, the loose end passed either between two boards of a fence if outdoors, or through the crack between the door and the door jam if indoors. The dog is then drawn tight up against the stationary object while a muzzle is applied. If an assistant is available, two lassos can be used, with each person drawing one tight in opposite directions, thus immobilizing the dog. One lasso is tied to a solid object, and while the assistant controls the other one to restrain the dog, the muzzle can be applied.

The dog that continues to struggle, even after he has been muzzled, may be restrained by tying his front legs and hind legs together. The object of restraining a dog is to prevent him from doing damage to himself and to protect the person who is administering first aid. A small dog can frequently be restrained by tossing a blanket over him and gathering him up in that.

Broken Bones

This is probably the most common injury requiring emergency first aid treatment. Broken bones are known as fractures and there are two types: simple fractures in which the bone is broken but the ends remain inside the skin of the body, and compound fractures, where the ends of the bone protrude through the skin. Of the two, the latter is far more serious but both should be set by a skilled veterinarian as soon as possible.

It is frequently difficult to determine whether a dog's leg has been broken or is merely injured, bruised, sprained or pulled. This is because when a dog feels pain in its leg it will limp regardless of how serious or trivial the cause. Feel the leg gently for suspicious bumps or dislocations. If in doubt, run your hand along the other leg at the same location to see whether the two feel the same. If there is any question in your mind, splint the leg until the services of a veterinarian can be obtained. He will have X-ray equipment and be in a better position to judge whether an actual break has occurrred.

The simplest type of splint consists of two sticks (even broken tree branches will do in an emergency) which are laid on either side of the leg and then tied securely above and below the suspected break. This keeps the dog from moving or thrashing his leg about as any action can cause the broken ends of bone to penetrate the skin and perhaps sever an important blood vessel. If supplies are at hand, it is best to wrap the leg in absorbent cotton before applying the splints. The splints can be fastened in place by putting additional layers of cotton about them and wrapping the entire leg carefully with a bandage. This makes a much more secure splint and will hold the leg firmly in place until the bone can be set. Occasionally a dog's tail will be broken and the same procedure should be followed. It is not uncommon to see a dog with a kinked tail due to a break which was not set at the time of injury.

Sprains

Puppies are prone to sprains or strains – twisting a leg when playing, falling in a hole, all sorts of things. You may well hear a frightful scream, rush to see what is the matter, and have your puppy "tell you" he has hurt his leg and will never be able to walk again. Take him away from his companions at once. Keep him alone and quiet, and very often after a short period you will find him perfectly all right. However, if this does not happen, there are various liniments and remedies, nearly all of them to be found in the family medicine chest.

Should it be necessary to bandage your dog, this may present a problem, because he may try to tear it off. If he does, cover the outside of the bandage with hot mustard. This should end any idea he may have of chewing it. However, I once had a dog who liked the taste of mustard, so in his case I used bitter aloes. This soon stopped the gentleman! An Elizabethan "ruff" made of cardboard will help to prevent this also.

One word of warning concerning bandages. If the dog seems to be in pain after a bandage has been applied, check that it is not on too tight; for although it may have been all right when applied, it is possible for an injured part to swell, causing the bandage to tighten.

Bruises

A dog does not seem to suffer as quickly and easily from bruising as does a human being. The best advice is to give the dog rest and to keep the bruised area cool, by the application of either ice packs or cold compresses. Unless a bone has been chipped, this treatment will usually be quite sufficient, and the trouble should clear up in a matter of days.

Eye Accidents

It is all too easy for a dog to injure its eye. Puppy may scratch puppy; an adult dog at work or play can very easily run onto a spike or a sharp twig.

If your dog comes to you with an eye closed and tearing, examine it for a foreign body. This is usually easy to deal with. Hold the dog's head slightly to one side, and raise its lower eyelid just enough to make a tiny cup. Into this pour lukewarm water or cold tea, and try to flush out the object. If this fails, take the dog to your veterinarian as quickly as you can, before the foreign body does more injury.

A scratch on the eye is another matter. The best thing to use is penicillin ointment, if you have some (a prescription is required), putting some into the eye; then take your dog to the veterinarian. If no ointment is available, wash the eye out with lukewarm water before rushing the dog to the vet.

Stings

A puppy chasing a lazy bee or even a wasp, which he will consider a grand thing to play with, may well end up with a nasty sting. Remember that a bee leaves its sting in the animal; a wasp does not. Because of the density of a Collie's coat, stings on the body are rare, but stings on the muzzle, ear, tongue, eye, and throat are quite common. Stings in the throat (when the insect is swallowed) are particularly dangerous because if the throat swells up it may cause suffocation. If your dog is stung and starts to swell, look well into the spot to find the center; and if you can find a sting, remove it with tweezers. Then apply cut onion or a little bicarbonate of soda. If the sting is in the mouth, it is not necessary to make a paste of the bicarbonate – just rub it on. If not, make the bicarbonate into a thick paste before applying it. Watch your dog until you are quite certain that the swelling is not increasing. If it does, particularly in the mouth or throat, take him to your veterinarian at once.

Wounds

A dog can very easily be wounded – minor cuts, scratches, or bites from another dog – but these rarely require treatment because the dog's tongue will usually do all that is necessary to keep such wounds clean until they are healed. A wound that bleeds freely is generally safe because it will rid itself of any poisons. The kind of wound which can be dangerous is a deep puncture wound which bleeds little or not at all, and tends to heal from the surface inwards, trapping bacteria and becoming septic at a later stage. This type of wound should be kept open until it appears absolutely clean and healthy.

Before bandaging any wound, make sure there is no foreign body in it; and if there is, do your very best to extract it. If you cannot do so, get professional help. Wounds should be bathed with a mild antiseptic solution after the hair has been cut away from the area. Penicillin ointment, although obtainable only on prescription, is excellent for all wounds so it is wise to keep some in your medicine chest. A large cut may need suturing, and for this, of course, you will have to see your vet. If a wound is bleeding excessively, it may be necessary to apply a tourniquet, or to try to stop the bleeding with a pressure bandage.

Tourniquet

Cuts in the limbs frequently bleed far out of proportion to the actual injury. However, any extensive loss of blood is, of course, dangerous and a tourniquet should be applied. Any piece of strong cloth or cord will do to make a tourniquet; even a handkerchief, or a necktie. Before applying a tourniquet, you must decide whether the blood is coming from a vein or an artery. Arterial blood will be bright red and come out in a pulsing beat; venous blood will be dark and flow more steadily. It is important to determine which type of blood vessel has been cut, because to stop arterial bleeding you must apply the tourniquet between the artery cut and the heart; whereas to stop the flow of blood from the vein, the tourniquet should be applied on the far side of the cut from the heart. Take your piece of cord or cloth and tie it around the limb loosely, tying a secure knot. A small piece of stick is then inserted through the loop and twisted to tighten the cord until the flow of blood stops. The tourniquet should be loosened every five to ten minutes to prevent loss of circulation from permanently damaging the limb.

Pressure Bandage

A pressure bandage is a bandage which is applied over the injury tightly enough to stop the flow of blood. Apply a pad of absorbent cotton to the affected area. Wrap this tightly with regular gauze bandage and then cover the area with adhesive tape to keep the dog from chewing it off. Applied tightly enough, it will stop the bleeding.

Inexperienced people frequently apply pressure bandages without tightening them enough to actually do the job for which they are intended. Because of this necessary tightness, such bandages should not be left on for more than 15 to 20 minutes. If applied to the foot because of a cut in or about the pad, a pressure bandage can be left in place for as long as thirty minutes.

Shock

A dog in any accident, especially one that involves a blow to the head, or one in which some vital organ is damaged or ribs broken will generally, mercifully, go into shock. He is less conscious of pain, but his condition is often frightening, his pulse and respiration slow and often shallow. He may feel cold to the touch, pant, have a rapid pulse, and exhibit extreme thirst.

Don't try to apply a lot of heat. The best treatment is to cover the dog with blankets and let his own body heat build up. Don't try to move him, unless the weather is extermely cold, or unless he is in the direct sun which is too hot for him. In that case, place an open blanket on the groud alongside him and try to roll or slide him onto it; then, using the blanket as a stretcher, carry him to a more suitable location, or to where he can obtain professional help. Should he seem conscious, and desirous of drinking, you may spoon-feed him, but very slowly to allow him a chance to swallow naturally. Make some instant coffee – such as you would drink yourself, add Karo or honey (75 $\%$ coffee to 25 $\%$ syrup) and a pinch of salt. Try to hold his head up so that he can swallow naturally, but if he struggles or resists swallowing, discontinue the spoon-feeding. The caffeine in coffee is a natural stimulant but a mild one, and the syrup contains glucose which provides energy.

While he is in shock you may be able to get him to a veterinarian who will be able to sedate him; as the state of shock disappears, the dog becomes more conscious of pain.

If a small dog is in shock, pick him up by holding one hand under his front, and the other under his hindquarters. This will help to keep him stretched out.

Artificial Respiration

After an accident, a dog is sometimes unable to breathe. Should yours be in this condition, first pull his tongue out and, if unconscious, wipe out his throat with cotton or your handkerchief. Feel for a heartbeat and if you can detect it, try gently pressing on the rib cage and quickly releasing the pressure. Repeat many times, rhythmically, about twenty times to the minute. Stop as soon as you see or feel him breathing normally. This procedure has saved many a dog.

Collapse

Collapse usually occurs in an old dog. It may happen on a very hot day; if it does, move him to the coolest place you can find, making sure he is in a current of fresh air. Check that his tongue is clear of his windpipe; pull it out of his mouth, and let it hang so that there is no chance of his swallowing it. Raise him and keep his head a little lower than his body, and send for your veterinarian.

Should the collapse occur in cold weather keep the dog as warm as possible while awaiting the arrival of your vet, taking the same precautions with his tongue.

Electric Shock

The wire on the floor offers temptation to any dog, and especially to puppies. If your puppy persists in going behind the furniture or remaining quietly out of sight, check and make sure that he is not lying there gnawing on a lamp wire. If he chews through the insulation, his mouth will be badly burned, sometimes severely. He may urinate, and if he is standing close to a metal conductor which the urine touches he may well be electrocuted.

If this happens, keep away from the urine and shut off the switch which feeds the wire. If you rush to his aid without taking this precaution, you, too, may be electrocuted. If you cannot for any reason shut off the current, use a dry wooden object to remove the wire from the dog's mouth, or to push the dog away from the live wire. If he has stopped breathing, try giving artificial respiration, as explained above. He will probably be in shock. Treat him accordingly. If his tongue or lips are burned, take him to the doctor. Remember, puppies and exposed wires do not go well together, so try always to keep them apart, particularly when the puppy is going through his "chewing" stage as his new teeth come in.

Drowning

This is rare. Dogs swim naturally and have no problem in the water. However, they sometimes fall or are pushed off a height and the impact either with the water, or an object in the water, may render them unconscious, and they drown. Another cause of accidental drowning is when children play with dogs and try to ride them or climb on their backs in the water.

The first thing to do is to pull the dog's tongue and shake his head in a lowered position to drain out as much excess water as possible.

As soon as possible, apply artificial respiration; this will frequently save a life. The important thing is to sense the urgency. Deliberate speed may very well determine whether your dog lives or dies.

Heat Stroke

The only appreciable way a dog has of reducing his temperature is by evaporating water from his throat, tongue, and footpads. He has few sweat glands such as a human being has. That is why a dog pants, and when extremely hot, salivates as well. As the water evaporates, he becomes cold at the point of evaporation. To reduce a dog's temperature to normal, we must put this principle to work.

Suppose you find your dog panting and slobbering in a state of collapse? How do you give first aid? The quickest way is to put him in the bathtub and run cold water over him. Should there be no bathtub available, you may use a hose, and, lacking even that, dashing a bucket of cold water over him will help. With the dog thoroughly soaked, try to provide circulation of air around him. An electric fan is probably the best means, but again, if this is not available, a flapping cardboard or towel, or even a newspaper used as a fan will keep the air moving and help reduce his body temperature. The important thing is not to slacken in your efforts until the dog shows definite signs of recovery.

Should you be driving at the time heat prostration strikes – a frequent occurrence – lay the dog on the floor of the front seat, wet him down and keep the hood ventilator open to let the air flow over him while you drive. Continue to pour enough water over his body to keep him damp on the way to help. If you are driving across a hot desert area and your dog can't stand heat, be sure to prepare yourself in advance with containers of water.

The important thing to remember is to get the dog out of the heated area as soon as possible into a shaded place and to circulate air around him while wetting him down.

Fish Hooks

It is not unusual for a dog to be hooked, particularly when a lure is snapped back preparatory to casting over the water. Do not try to pull the hook back out of the skin the way it entered, as the barb will tear the flesh. Fortunately, most fishing boxes contain hook cutting pliers. Should none be available at the moment, cut the line fastened to the hook, and try to keep the dog from struggling until pliers can be obtained. Cut the shank of the hook as close to the skin as possible, and pull each half out. The wound can be treated as indicated under *Wounds*.

Porcupine Quills

Collies sometimes encounter porcupines and end up stuck with quills. It usually happens in a place far from veterinary help. So if you are going into woods known to be porcupine country better take along a pair of electricians' pliers. First chain the dog and hold him standing while you pull the quills from one side – pull! no matter how painful. He can then be laid on that side. Work on his mouth next, and his tongue. Then around his eyes. Next behind the shoulders and the belly to prevent quills from working into vital organs. Consider this merely first aid. Get the dog to the vet's as fast as possible. Quills that work themselves in will have to be removed under anesthetic.

Splinters

When you see your dog limping, examine the pads, particularly between them, for splinters or thorns which may have become imbedded in the flesh. If the head is visible, tie the dog's mouth so that he cannot snap from pain, and pull the object out with a strong pair of tweezers by taking a firm grip of the splinter, as close to the flesh as you can. If it does not come right out, removing it is a job for the veterinarian. Splinters left in the flesh too long can cause tetanus (lockjaw), especially if pus develops. Your dog's doctor will decide whether to give antitoxin.

Not all splinters enter the feet. The dog will show you the offender when he tries to pull it out.

Skunk Spray

Dogs allowed to wander freely, even in the suburbs, frequently meet a skunk, with the inevitable result. While it is true that time and weather will take care of the odor, the dog, who will be quite a bit upset and come galloping home, cannot be allowed to remain in his odorous state about the house. Frequently, the eyes are irritated by the spray. Fortunately, skunk spray causes only local irritation – never blindness.

To remove the odor, wash your dog with a detergent, rinse him well, and then rub canned tomato or orange juice into the coat. Allow it to soak in for at least ten minutes, then rebathe him with a strong detergent, and rinse. You may have to repeat this procedure several times because, no doubt about it, skunk odor lingers!

Poisoning

When poisoning is suspect, the first thing to do is to determine the kind of poison involved. For instance, if you see your pet dig up mole bait, quickly locate the container and read the formula. Only when you know your poison can you supply the proper antidote. The wrong antidote can even intensify the effects of the poison. But in almost all cases, the first thing to do is to empty the dog's stomach while someone else phones the vet for advice. (Many of the larger cities have Poison Control Centers. They are listed in the phone book – if not call your Department of Health – and they will give you advice over the phone in an emergency).

Hydrogen peroxide is an excellent – and usually handy – emetic. Use a 3% solution (this is the common household strength) mixed half and half with water. Feed it to the dog a spoonful at a time so he won't choke – one tablespoon of the mixture for each ten pounds of dog.

Some poisons are corrosive; they burn what they touch: mouth, throat, gullet, stomach. In such cases, unless antidotes are given almost immediately, it is too late. Because the stomach contains fluid, the damage by some acids and alkalis is not quite so immediate. The way to counteract their damage is to try to keep the poisons from corroding deeper into tissue and to neutralize them.

Once an area has been damaged, it requires a long time to heal. The dog may be unable to eat for weeks, yet continue to live. Any treatment given while the dog is recuperating must take this into consideration. Don't expect your vet to wave a wand and heal all the damaged tissue. No, it will take time and you must be a patient nurse all through the healing process.

Here are some of the more common poisons:

Alkalis: The most frequent one is drain cleaner. When cleaning drains some of the leftover caustic is frequently thrown into the garbage. It takes only a few crystals to cause damage. *Symptoms:* Intense salivation, often followed by nausea and vomiting, and expression of pain. *Treatment:* Neutralize the caustic by giving vinegar or lemon juice.

Garbage Poisoning: Partially decomposed food in which food poisoning organisms have developed can be deadly, but there is often time to save the dog. *Symptoms:* Usually trembling is the first sign, followed by prostration. When botulin poisoning is the cause, the dog becomes slack all over as if he lacked strength in his muscles, especially the neck. Frequently he is unable to vomit voluntarily. *Treatment:* Empty the stomach with peroxide diluted by half with water, and when the nausea has ended, give Epsom salts or another quick acting laxative.

Cyanide: Many cyanide poisonings are deliberate, but not always. Because so many suburbanites are troubled by ground moles, thousands of packages of mole poisons are sold annually. The property owner buries them in burrows to kill the moles. But, unfortunately, curious dogs see or smell the place where the ground has been freshly dug, scratch up the mole poison and eat it. Many mole poisons contain cyanide, but not enough of it to be immediately fatal. *Symptoms:* If you think your dog has swallowed cyanide, take a sniff of his breath: the odor of almonds will be smelled. Look to see if his gums and tongue are blue. He will show pain, and have trouble breathing. *Treatment:* Give peroxide (half and half) with water, and you may save him. But let your veterinarian carry on from there.

Warfarin: This most common of all rat poisons, fortunately for dog owners, must be eaten three or four times to cause death. Death is caused by internal bleeding. Even two times will cause some ill effects. *Symptoms:* Paleness of the gums, lips and tongue. General overall weakness. *Treatment:* In the early stages, simply keeping the dog away from warfarin will help him to recover. In the last stages, no treatment is known. Transfusions have been given but they produce only temporary improvement. Consult your veterinarian. In time, an antidote or more effective treatment may be discovered.

Phosphorus: Another common rodent poison. Its effects on dogs are cruel. *Symptoms:* Often causes writhing pain. The breath has a garlic odor; diarrhea begins rapidly; the dog first becomes prostrated, goes into a coma and dies. *Treatment:* Phosphorus circulating in the bloodstream damages internal organs. The quickest possible treatment is essential. Peroxide, mixed with water (half and half) is the antidote; it also causes vomiting. Even though you save your dog's life, it may be a long time before he will act like his old self.

Thallium: One of the commonest insect and rodent poisons. It is a slow poison with symptoms sometimes developing days after ingestion, at which time only supportive veterinary treatment is effective. *Symptoms:* When large amounts have been ingested, salivation and drooling, nausea and vomiting, diarrhea and expressions of pain. *Treatment:* A solution of table salt given as quickly as possible.

Paint: This is a broad term. The active poisons are the pigments used in their formulas and the lead in the white lead which gives paint substance and adhesive properties. Paris Green is sometimes used as a pigment. This is an arsenical, so any dog that licks fresh green paint should be considered a possible poison victim and be properly treated. The lead in the paint (if it is a lead-base paint) will complicate the problem. *Symptoms:* Tell-tale paint around the dog's muzzle and lips, or even on the body, should make one suspicious. He will exhibit pain in the abdomen, perhaps tremble, breathe rapidly and constantly move about until he becomes prostrate. *Treatment:* Empty the stomach, and when the nausea has subsided give a teaspoonful of Epsom salts in water. The lead is less dangerous, but the arsenic in the Paris Green may, if much has been absorbed, lengthen the period of convalescence.

Strychnine: Those who use strychnine to poison foxes or other varmints not infrequently accidentally poison dogs. But, like cyanide, strychnine poisoning is sometimes done maliciously. *Symptoms:* The typical violent twitching and trembling, with short periods of quiet can never be forgotten by anyone who has seen a dog with strychnine poisoning. These tremblings usually end in death, depending on the quantity of poison consumed. *Treatment:* If you can get your dog to the veterinarian alive, chances are that he can save him. He will inject a drug that will counteract the trembling and empty the stomach.

If you happen to have some sleeping capsules – one of the barbiturates ($1\frac{1}{2}$ gr.) such as phenobarbital, Nembutal or Seconal, dissolve the contents of five or six (if the dog is an adult Collie) in a little water, and administer it by the lip-pocket method. Then hurry to the veterinarian, if he cannot come to you.

Copper: Copper is occasionally eaten in the form of copper sulphate. Dogs chew corroded areas on copper pipes and become sick. Ingredients in some spray materials are also copper sulphate. *Symptoms:*

Expression of pain, sometimes convulsions, twitching; and after a lapse of time the dog may void blue-colored stools. *Treatment:* Use diluted peroxide to induce vomiting if you can treat the pet immediately, and then get him to the vet's – fast.

Plant Sprays: Today these consist of a wide variety of chemicals, and new ones are coming on the market every year. For some there are no antidotes. The old sprays were mostly arsenicals or copper sulphate, discussed above.

Insect Sprays: For DDT there is no published antidote.

Chlordane: Sprinkled on lawns or gardens to kill grubs, or spread around the foundations of homes to eradicate termites, it is an ever present danger. It is a slower poison than some. If you can't get to a veterinarian at once, induce vomiting with diluted peroxide.

Sodium Fluoride: This is sprinkled on floors and shelves of closets to destroy roaches and ants. Dogs often drop bones or meat on it, then eat the meat and are poisoned. Induce vomiting with peroxide in water, and get your dog to the vet.

Ant Cups or Buttons: These are used to rid premises of these annoying pests. Ant cups are metal bottle caps filled with a sweetened, poisoned material. Dogs often chew them, sometimes swallowing the caps along with the poison. They are usually made with thallium or arsenic so read the contents on the package label and give the proper antidote. Fortunately, both of these poisons are now being replaced with safer ones.

Radiator Antifreeze: It is often ethylene glycol. It may drip from a leak, and since it tastes sweet, dogs are tempted to lap it up. It changes to oxalic acid which does the real poisoning. *Symptoms:* Chiefly pain and nausea. *Treatment:* If you are sure the dog has lapped antifreeze, empty his stomach with diluted peroxide, and give a teaspoonful of bicarbonate of soda dissolved in water; then consult your veterinarian.

Chocolate: The theobromine in black cooking chocolate, similar to caffeine in coffee, is highly concentrated. Many dogs have stolen and eaten bars of this chocolate which, while it may not have proved fatal, produced violent shaking. *Treatment:* Empty the stomach with diluted peroxide and if you have any barbiturate sleeping pills dissolve the contents of several in an ounce of water. Don't exceed a 1½ grain capsule for each ten pounds of the dog's weight. Administer by the lip-pocket method. Then let your veterinarian carry on. He may inject a sedative intravenously and quickly counteract the nervous symptoms. Be sure to tell him what medication you have already given.

Laurel and Rhododendron Leaves: It is surprising how often dogs have been poisoned by these plants. No one has been able to discover the attraction. *Symptoms:* Nausea soon develops. There is profuse salivation and a general weakness. *Treatment:* Even if you know the dog has vomited, induce more vomiting with a peroxide mixture. Follow with Epsom salts for a laxative.

Sleeping Pills: It may surprise you to learn that many dogs somehow manage to find and eat sleeping pills. They must swallow them whole or the bitterness would cause the drug to be rejected. *Symptoms:* Should your dog for no apparent reason go into a deep sleep, suspect barbiturate poisoning. *Treatment:* Before he is too deeply unconscious to swallow, empty his stomach with diluted peroxide and give him half a cup of strong black coffee. Then take him to the veterinarian.

Choking

A dog may choke from an obstruction in his throat. If it is high up in the throat, suffocation may follow very quickly, so action is essential. Open the dog's mouth and try to pull out whatever has become lodged. If you fail, try very gently to push the object further down. If it goes into the lower part of the throat, the risk of imminent death is over. It may mean that the object will have to be surgically removed later, but at least you have a live dog from which to remove it. Other than this there is not much you can do in the case of the dog's choking. Take instant, speedy action.

Burns and Scalds

Unless the damaged area is slight, never attempt to treat a burn yourself. Cover the area with a loose bandage. Treat the dog for shock and take him at once to your vet. Your main object should be to exclude all air from the burnt area.

With Collies, scalds are more difficult to treat than burns, because the dog's thick coat holds in the heat from the boiling liquid. The best thing is to douse the dog immediately with lukewarm water; if necessary slosh a pot of lukewarm water over the affected area. Treat for shock and call in your veterinarian.

Love!

In Conclusion

Sometimes one fails to see the forest for the trees. This is particularly true when reading (or writing) a book like this. One becomes so concerned with facts and problems it is easy to lose sight of the whole.

Yet if one is to keep a Collie – or for that matter, any dog – there must be a reason. As we have seen, it is certainly not for financial profit. As a protector? Well, yes a dog like a Collie – powerful, alert and courageous – certainly makes a fine guardian of the home. For the children, to teach them selfless love and responsibility, as well as to provide a playmate? Yes, these too are good reasons.

And yet there is more than that, particularly when selecting a Collie. He has a rascal look, a gamin look, a look compounded of gaiety, love devotion, and an infectious sense of humor. He will sense and reflect your every mood – never obtrusive, ever present, ready to please you.

His beauty of appearance, unequalled by any dog, is more than matched by his beauty of soul. Oh yes, I do believe he has a soul. If he did not have one to begin with, well then, certainly somewhere along the way he must have acquired one as a reward for his long and meritorious companionship and service to man.

I think it was best summed up by Senator George Vest of Missouri. While defending Old Drum, a hound accused of killing sheep, he delivered this never to be forgotten tribute:

"Gentlemen of the Jury: The best friend a man has in this world may turn against him and become his enemy. His son or daughter that he has reared with loving care may prove ungrateful. Those who are nearest and dearest to us, those whom we trust with our happiness and our good name may become traitors to their faith. The money that a man has, he may lose. It flies away from him, perhaps in a moment of ill-considered action. The people who are prone to fall on their knees to do us honor when success is with us, may be the first to throw the stone of malice when failure settles its cloud upon our head.

"The one absolutely unselfish friend that man can have in this selfish world, the one that never deserts him, the one that never proves ungrateful or treacherous, is his dog. A man's dog stands by him in prosperity and in poverty, in health and in sickness. He will sleep on the cold ground, where the wintry winds blow and the snow drives fiercely, if only he may be near to his master's side. He will kiss the hand that has no food to offer; he will lick the wounds and sores that come in encounter with the roughness of the world. He guards the sleep of his pauper master as if he were a prince. When all other friends desert, he remains. When riches take wings and reputation falls to pieces, he is as constant in his love as the sun in its journey through the heavens.

"If fortune drives the master forth an outcast in the world, friendless and homeless, the faithful dog asks no higher privilege than that of accompanying him, to guard him against danger, to fight against his enemies. And when the last scene of all comes, and death takes his master in its embrace and his body is laid away, there by the graveside, will the noble dog be found, his head between his paws, his eyes sad, but open in alert watchfulness, faithful and true even in death."

Appendix—Dog Talk

Through the years dog aficionados have developed their own jargon. Some of these terms, such as "blocky" have passed into everyday speech; others, such as "apron" or "balance", are commonly used words adapted to dog purposes.

Use of such words in doggy conversation is almost mandatory for the dog lover. Understanding of their meaning will contribute to his enjoyment of dog books and articles.

The author has endeavored to minimize the use of dog world jargon in this book. However, some of the terms are so beautifully descriptive that they could not be omitted.

While not all of the terms defined in the glossary apply to Collies, they are included because a dog lover does not restrict his affection and understanding to one breed; his love embraces them all.

Affixes:	These are names usually attached to a dog's registered name so that it can be identified.
Almond-eyes:	Eyes set in tissue of almond shape.
Angulations:	Angles formed where the bones meet: shoulder, upper arm, hock, stifle.
Apple-head:	A head which is rounded on top of the skull as in the Toy Spaniels. An undesirable feature in most breeds.
Apron:	The frill or long hair below the neck on long-coated dogs.
Bad doer:	A dog who does badly however well fed and cared for. Often one who has never done well from birth.
Bad show-er:	A dog who will not or cannot display himself well at shows. May be due to contrariness, nerves or boredom.
Balance:	Coordination of the muscles giving graceful action coupled with the overall conformation of the dog.
	The lateral dimensions of the dog should mold pleasingly with the horizontal and vertical dimensions.
Barrel:	Refers to the rib cage. This should be strong

	and well-rounded, permitting plenty of heart room. The opposite to ribs that are flat-sided, lacking spring.
Bat ear	Large erect ears like those of a bat, as in the French Bulldog. A fault in many other breeds.
Bay:	The voice of a hound on the trail.
B.B.:	Best of Breed abbreviation.
Beard:	The profuse, rather bushy whiskers of the Brussels Griffon, not the terrier.
Beefy:	Heavy development of the hindquarters.
Belton:	The blue and white and orange and white-flecked color seen in certain English Setters. This is called ticking in Beagles.
Bench show:	Dog show where the dogs competing are "benched" or leashed on benches.
Bitchy:	Refers to an effeminate or ultrarefined male dog.
Bite:	Relative position of the lower and upper teeth when mouth is shut.
Blaze:	A white (usually bulbous) marking running up the center of the face of some dogs.
Blocky:	Term used to describe a head which is cube-shaped, as in the Boston Terrier.
Bloom:	Glossiness or good sheen of coat, especially desirable in a smoothcoated breed.
Blue:	A blue-gray, such color as might be seen in the Whippet or Bedlington.
Bobtail:	A naturally tailless dog. Often used for the Old English Sheepdog.
Bone:	A well-boned dog is one having limbs giving an appearance and feel of strength and spring without coarseness.
Br.:	Breeder, that is the owner of the dog's dam at the time of whelping.
B.R. or br.:	Blue Roan, a mixture of blue and white in which the colors are blended about equally.
Brace:	Two dogs or two dogs exhibited together.
Breeching:	The tan hairs on the backs and thighs of such a breed as the Manchester Terrier.

234

Brindle:	A mixture of dark and light hairs giving a generally dark effect, usually being lighter streaks on a gray, tawny, brown or black background. Found in Scottish Terriers and the Bull breeds especially.
Brisket:	That part of the body in front of the chest and between the forelegs.
Broken Color:	Where the main coat color is broken-up by white or other hairs.
Broken-haired:	Roughed-up wiry coat.
Broken-up face:	Any face which shows a combination of lay-back, projecting lower jaw and wrinkle. Seen in the Pekingese, Bulldog and Pug.
Brood matron:	A female kept for breeding purposes.
B.S.:	Best in Show or Best in Sex. A dog who has beaten all others or all others in his sex, respectively.
Brush:	A tail which has long bushy hair such as seen in the Spitz breeds.
Burr:	The irregular formation inside the ear.
Butterfly Nose:	The nostrils are mottled or show flesh color among the black or brown pigment.
Button Ears:	Ears which drop over in front covering the inner cavity, such as in the Fox Terrier.
Bye:	After dogs have been paired at field trials, the odd dog remaining.
Cat foot:	A compact and round foot, well held together, like the foot of a cat.
C.C.:	Challenge Certificate. A Kennel Club award signed by the judge for the best dog of his breed at a Championship Show.
C.D.:	Companion Dog. One holding this degree has passed a test for obedience and character reliability.
C.D.X.:	Companion Dog (Excellent). A degree indicating that the holder has passed a test for obedience and character reliability.
Champion:	A dog that has been awarded his cham-

	pionship by the AKC after defeating a number of dogs in competitive judgings.
Character:	A combination of the essential points of appearance and disposition contributing to the whole, and distinctive to the particular variety of dog to which the holder belongs.
Cheeky:	Full, thick cheeks.
China Eye:	A blue, wall eye.
Choke collar:	A leather or chain collar that tightens or loosens according to the hand controlling it.
Chops:	The pendulous and upper lips common to the Bulldog and some hounds.
Cloddy:	A low and very thick-set build.
Chun Red:	A rich coppery shade popular in the Pekingese, named after the famous Champion "Goodwood Chun".
Close Coupled:	Short or closely knit between the last ribs and the hip joints.
Close Lying:	A coat, in which the body hair lies flat and snug on the body.
C.M.:	Certificate of Merit. An award to Field Trial competitors of outstanding merit but not prize winners.
Cobby:	Of compact, neat and muscular formation (like a cob horse).
Companion Dog (C.D.):	Also, Companion Dog Excellent (C.D.X.); Utility Dog (U.D.); Tracking Dog (T.D.); Titles awarded in Obedience Trials.
Condition:	General health, coat and appearance.
Conformation:	The form and structure and arrangement of parts in conformance with the Breed Standard.
Corky:	Compact, nimble in body and mind, lively and spirited.
Coupling:	That part of the body between the last ribs and the hip joints, joined by the backbone.

Couple:	Two hounds.
Cow-hocked:	A dog is said to be cow-hocked when his hocks are bent inwards, thus throwing the hind feet outwards. A fault in any breed, even in the Pyrenean Mountain Dog and present-day St. Bernard.
Crank-tail:	A screw tail.
Chest:	The upper arched part of a dog's neck.
Cropping:	The practice of cutting or trimming a dog's ears to make them small and/or erect in various defined shapes. The practice is common in Europe, but illegal in Britain and some American states.
Crossbred:	A dog whose parents are of different breeds.
Croup:	The area adjacent to the sacrum and immediately before the root of the tail.
Cryptorchid:	The adult dog whose testicles are abnormally retained in the abdominal cavity.
Culotte:	The feathery tail on the back of the forelegs of the Pekingese, Pomeranian and Schipperke.
Cushion:	The fullness of the foreface given by the padding of the upper lips in the Mastiff and Bulldog.
D or d:	The abbreviation for the male dog as described in show catalogs, race cards, etc.
Dam:	The female parent of puppies. The term is generally used but has special reference to a bitch from the time of her whelping a litter to the weaning of her last puppy in that litter.
Dappled:	A term usual in Dachshunds. It means a variegated or mottled color; usually small, confluent blotches of silver with tan, black or black-and-tan.
Derby:	Field trail competition for young dogs.
Dewclaws:	The rudimentary fifth digit and claws found on the insides of the legs below the hocks, which are better removed a few days after birth.

Dewlap:	The loose pendulous skin under the throat as in the Bloodhound.
Dimples:	The shallow depressions at each side of the breastbone, as in the Dachshund.
Dish-faced:	When a depression in the nasal bone makes the nose higher in the tip than at the top.
Docking:	Shortening the dog's tail by amputation.
Dome:	The term which refers to the rounded skull of some dogs, as the Spaniel.
Double coat:	The outer coat is weather-resistant and protective. Inner coat is of softer hair for warmth.
Down-faced:	When the tip of the nose curves well below the level of the stop. Opposite to dish-faced.
Down in Pastern	Showing an angle of the front feet forward and outward instead of straight in line from the forearm to the ground in those breeds which require this formation.
Drop Ears:	Ears which are pendant and hanging close and flat to the side of the cheek.
Dual Champion:	In England this is one who has not only reached Championship status in the show ring but has qualified for a working certificate as a gundog in the field. In America such a dog would be known as a "bench and field champion".
Dudley Nose:	Wholly flesh-color nostrils, usually cherry or coffee-colored; quite distinct from Butterfly Nose.
Elbow:	The joint at the top of the forearm.
Elbows-out:	Elbows not close to the body, as those of the Bulldog. A fault in most other breeds.
Expression:	A combination of the position, size, color and luster of the eyes, giving the countenance the desired distinction peculiar to the particular variety of dog.
Fall:	The long hair overhanging the face in the Skye and Yorkshire Terriers.

False Heat:	Not uncommon in bitches. The animal will give every sign of expecting, even experiencing a heat, but these will not persist for the length of time of a normal period and she will revert or "go off" very quickly. When a bitch with a false heat is mated it usually proves unfruitful.
Fancier:	One who is actively interested in some phase of dogdom.
Feather, Featherings:	The long hair fringing on the back of the legs of some breeds such as Spaniels and Setters. The term is loosely applied to include ear fringes and tail flag.
Felted:	When a coat becomes matted.
Fetch:	To retrieve.
Fiddle Head:	A long wolfish head.
Field Trial:	Competition in which dogs are judged on ability in following a trail or retrieving game.
Filled-up Face:	One in which the cheek muscles are well developed, such as in the Staffordshire.
Flag:	The long, fine, silky hairs under the tails of Setters and some Retrievers, graduating in length from long at the root to short at the tip of the tail.
Flank:	Side between the last rib and hip.
Flecked:	When the coat is lightly ticked with another color, yet not roaned, spotted or dappled.
Flews:	The pendulous inner corners of the lips of the upper jaw.
Frill:	The hair under the neck and on the chest.
Fringes:	See Feathering.
Fly-ears:	Semi-erect ears which stand out from the side of the head.
Front:	Strictly speaking all that can be seen from the front exept the head, but having special reference to the brisket and forelegs.
Forelock:	The abundant tassle of hair grown on the forehead, which falls over towards the eyes

	rather like a cap, such as in the Kerry Blue Terrier.
Frog-face:	A face in which the nose is extended and the jaw recedes, with special reference to short-face breeds.
Furrow:	The groove or indentation running in a median line from the stop to near the occiput.
Gait:	How a dog walks, trots or runs.
Gay Tail:	One which from root to tip is carried above the horizontal.
Good Doer:	A dog who does well without any special treatment, and who has thrived from birth.
Good Show-er:	A dog who displays himself to perfection at the show regardless of his general condition.
Goose-Rump:	A sloping croup which falls away too abruptly, the tail being set on too low.
Groups:	The six divisions into which the AKC has grouped all breeds: Sporting Dogs; Hounds; Working Dogs; Terriers; Toys; Non-Sporting Dogs.
Guide Dog:	A dog trained to guide blind people. Usually a bitch of the German Shepherd, Retriever, Airedale or Collie breeds.
Gun-shy:	A dog which is fearful at the sight of a gun or its report.
Gun-dog:	Dog trained to find live game and retrieve it when shot.
Handler:	A person who handles dogs at shows. It applies to any one who does this, but it usually refers to a professional or highly trained handler.
Hard-mouthed:	A dog is said to be hard-mouthed when he damages the game he retrieves. The term is in special reference to Gun-dogs.
Hare Feet:	Feet which are rather long and narrow with the toes well separated as in the Hare.
Harlequin:	Pied or patched black and white coat, referring specially to a type of Great Dane.

Haw:	An inner eye-lid more developed in some breeds than in others. It hangs open and shows red in such breeds as the Great Dane and Bloodhound.
H.C.:	Highly Commended. An award granted to an exhibit of outstanding merit but which generally carries with it no monetary award and stands sixth in placing.
Heat:	A bitch is said to be "in heat" during her oestral period, when she is in season, or menstruating.
Height:	The height of a dog is usually measured perpendicularly from the ground to the withers, i.e. to the top of the shoulders.
H.M.:	Hound Marked. When the body patches conform to the conventional pattern of hounds, i.e., a dark saddle (usually black), dark ears and head (usually tan), and often a patch about the set-on or on the upper limbs, the rest of the dog being white.
Hocks:	The joints in the hind legs between the pasterns and stifles, similar to the ankle in humans.
Huckle Bones:	The top of the hip joints.
Inbreeding:	The mating of closely related dogs. This is done to perpetuate certain characteristics which are considered desirable and which already exist to some extent. (See relevant paragraph).
Int. Ch.:	International Champion. A dog who has been awarded the title of champion in more than one country. It is not an officially recognized term by The Kennel Club.
Keel:	The absolute base of a Dachshund body with special reference to the brisket.
Kink-Tail:	A tail with a break or a kink in it.
Layback:	The receding nose found in some of the short-faced breeds.
Leash:	A thong by which dogs are held. An obsolete term for three Greyhounds.

Leather:	The skin of the ear-flap. It is sometimes trimmed to make neat or to prevent a hound from getting his ears torn.
Leggy:	So high in the leg that the dog appears assymetrical.
Level Jaws:	When the jaws are so placed that the teeth meet about evenly, neither undershot nor noticeably overshot.
Linebreeding:	The mating of dogs of similar strains not too closely related. (See relevant paragraph).
Lippy:	When the lips overhang or are developed more than they should.
Litter:	Collective term for the number of puppies born to the bitch at the same whelping.
Liver:	A color – deep reddish brown.
Loaded shoulders:	Heaviness in shoulders.
Loins:	That part of the body protecting the lower viscera, between the last ribs and hindquarters.
Long Coupled:	The reverse to close coupled. Dachshunds would be termed long coupled dogs.
Lumber:	Too much flesh, ungainly in appearance and clumsy in action. Does not apply to puppies.
Lurcher:	A crossbred hound.
Maiden:	In the general sense an un-mated bitch, but in exhibition world language a dog or bitch not having won a first-prize.
Mane:	An abundance of long hair around the top of the neck.
Mask:	The dark markings on the muzzle in some breeds, or the muzzle itself.
Match show:	A form of competition which is arranged more or less privately by members of local and breed societies to discuss and compare special points in the specimens presented.
Mating:	An act by which a bitch is served in co-

	pulation by a stud dog. A service.
Matron:	A brood bitch. One kept for breeding purposes.
Merle:	Bluish-grey color marbled with black, seen in working Sheepdogs.
Miscellaneous Class:	The class at dog shows for dogs of certain specified breeds for which no regular classification exists.
Molera:	Incomplete ossification of the skull. Characteristic of Chihuahuas.
Monorchid:	A dog with one descended testicle. See Cryptorchid.
Muzzle:	Foreface of the dog: nasal bone, nostrils, jaws. Also a strap or wire cage attached to the dog.
N.F.C.:	Not For Competition. Used when a dog is entered at a show purely for display not for competition.
Novice:	Generally an amateur or professional breeder of little experience. A beginner or tyro. Also a class distinction classification for a dog or bitch not having won two first prizes.
Occiput:	The part of the skull at the top of the back of the head which is prominent in most of the Hound group.
Oestrum:	The menstrual period. A bitch experiencing oestral flow is said to be "in heat" or "in season", that is, she is sexually excited and ripe for service by a male dog.
On His Toes:	The term indicates that a dog is alert and exhibiting himself well.
Otter Tail:	A tail which is thick at the roots and tapers away like that of an otter. Seen in some Retrievers.
Out At Elbows:	Having the joints of the elbow turned out and away from the side of the body, due to faulty front formation.
Outcross:	The mating of unrelated dogs or those of an entirely different strain (see relevant

paragraph).

Out At Shoulders:	Having the shoulders protruding outwards so as to increase the width of the front, as in the Bulldog.
Overshot:	Having the upper incisors projecting over and beyond the lower incisors.
Pace:	A gait which promotes a rolling motion of the body.
Pack:	Several hounds kept together. Mixed pack is made up of males and females.
Pad:	The cushioned sole of the foot.
Parti-color:	A coat of two or more colors in patches.
Pastern:	The lowest part of the leg, below the knee on the foreleg or below the hock on the hind leg.
Peak:	The term applied to the occiput when it is prominent, but rightly restricted to use with Basset Hounds, Bloodhounds and some Setters.
Pedigree:	A table of genealogy, giving the names of the dog's ancestors.
Pencilling:	The thin, dark elegant lines on the surface of the toes of some breeds, as in the English Toy Terrier.
Pied:	A term used for a dog having two coat colors in *unequal* proportions: mainly white with large black patches or brindle sections placed irregularly over the body. Sometimes referred to as Piebald. When the patches are golden or red brindle, the term used is Skewbald.
Pig-jaw:	Badly overshot jaw.
Pile:	The thick undercoat of a medium or long-coated dog.
Piley:	A coat that contains both soft and hard hair, as in the Dandie Dinmont Terrier.
Plume:	The soft hair on the tails of both the Pekingese and Pomeranian, this being long and feathery.
Pompon:	A rounded tuft of hair on the tail (Poodle).

	Sometimes miscalled Pom-Pom.
Prefix:	A particular kennel's name which is entered before a dog's name to identify it with that kennel.
Premium list:	An announcement sent to prospective exhibitors in a forthcoming dog show, containing list of awards.
Prick Ears:	Ears which stand erect.
Puppy:	A dog under 12 months of age.
Quarterings:	The junctions of the limbs, especially the hindquarters.
Racy:	Slight in build and rather longbodied.
Rangy:	Rather elongated in body and loose-limbed. Having rather more substance than one who is racy.
Red:	A general term for several colors, ranging from fallow or fawn down to copper.
Reserve:	Usually the fourth place after judging.
Ribbed Up:	A compact dog with the ribs nicely barrelled and placed.
Ring:	The area in which exhibits are handled and placed before a judge at the show. In most cases it is rectangular in spite of its name.
Ring Tail:	A curled tail which describes an almost complete circle.
Roach Back:	One that arches upwards from the withers along the spine, with particular emphasis about the loins.
Roan:	A mixture of white with another color (usually blue or red) in about equal proportions and showing good blending.
Rose Ears:	Ears which fold over, exposing the inner burr.
R.R. or r.r.:	Red Roan. A mixture of red and white in which the colors are blended about equally.
Ruff:	The frill or apron of long, stand-off hair, usually coarse, around the neck of some breeds, such as the Chow Chow.

Sable:	When the outer coat is shaded with black over a light undercoat, a dog is said to be of sable color, as in Collies.
Saddle:	A rectangular marking of black on the back extending to the upper flanks.
Sanction Show:	A show held under special rules for Members of a club and sanctioned by a Kennel Club.
Scent:	Odor left by an animal on the trail (ground scent) or wafted in the air (airborne scent).
Screw Tail:	A tail which is short and rapidly tapered to a point, and is twisted or screwed, as in some Bulldogs and Boston Terriers.
Season:	When a bitch menstruates she is said to be "in season".
Second Mouth:	A dog has his second mouth when the first or milk teeth are replaced by the second or permanent teeth.
Second Thighs:	The muscular development of the legs between the stifles and the hocks.
Self color:	One color or whole color except for lighter shadings.
Self-marked:	When a dog is all one color.
Semi-prick ears:	Ears carried erect with tips bending forward.
Septum:	The very thin dividing bone between the nostrils.
Service:	The term given to the act of copulation when a bitch is served by a stud dog. A "free service" is one given by courtesy of the owner of a stud dog following an unsuccessful service for which a fee has been paid.
Set-on:	Where the root of the tail is set on to the body.
Shelly:	Having a narrow and shallow body, but not necessarily lacking in bone and substance.
Shoulders:	The point at which the height of a dog is measured, about the top of the shoulder blades.

Sickle hocks:	Hocks which are both well let down and well bent, as in most racily built breeds.
Sickle tail:	One which describes a semi-circle and is usually gay.
Sire:	The male parent of a litter of puppies.
Sloping shoulders:	Those which are well laid back and therefore angulated to a more or less marked degree.
Smooth coat:	Short hair, close-lying.
Snipy:	When the dog's muzzle is weak and too long and narrow.
Soft mouth:	A dog with a soft mouth is one who can retrieve game without damaging it. It is especially applied to Gun-dogs.
Soundness:	The state of the dog's physical and mental health when everything is functioning normally.
Splay feet:	Those feet in which the toes are spread wide apart, as in some feet employed to work on marshy ground.
Spay:	A surgical operation to prevent conception.
Spread:	The distance covered by the wide-apart forelegs of a Bulldog. The exaggerated front of any out-at-shoulders dog.
Spring:	Elasticity. Spring of rib is when the ribs are well rounded, sound and elastic.
Squirrel tail:	One which curves forward over the back even from the root, as in some short-tailed terriers.
Stance:	Way of standing.
Standard:	The official description of the ideal dog, by which dogs are judged at shows.
Stand off:	The ruff or frill of rather coarse hair which stands off or away from the neck of some of the Spitz breeds.
Staring coat:	When the hair is dry, harsh, curling at the tips.
Stern:	The tail. A term used mainly in Beagle, Harrier, and Foxhound circles.

Stifle:	The joint in the hind leg joining the first and second thighs and corresponding to the human knee.
Sting:	A tail which is quite thin, even at the root, and tapers away to a fine point, as in the Irish Water Spaniel.
Stop:	The depression or stop between and in front of the eyes, approximating the bridge of the nose in humans.
Straight hocks:	Those which are practically vertical, lacking bend.
Straight shoulders:	Those which are not laid back and lack angulation.
Stud book:	A record of the breeding particulars of recognized breeds.
Stud dog:	A male dog kept partly or solely for breeding purposes and for whose services the owner charges a stud fee.
Sway back:	One which through spinal defects or poor muscular development sags in the middle.
Team:	Three or more dogs of one breed.
T.:	Ticked.
T.A.F.:	Transfer applied for.
T.D.:	Tracking dog. One who has passed a test in tracking work.
Throaty:	A dog is said to be throaty when he carries an excess of loose skin about the throat.
Thumb marks:	The round black spots on the forelegs about the pasterns on the Manchester Terrier and English Toy Terrier.
Ticked:	When small elongated specks of another color appear on the main body color.
Tie:	The term used in reference to the locking of dog and bitch during the mating union.
Tiger brindle:	A mixture of dark and light hairs among which the dark color forms a series of stripes or has the resemblance of stripes.
Timber:	Another name for bone. Good bone formation especially in the legs.
Tongue:	To give tongue is to give voice or bark.

Top-knot:	The long fluffy hair on the top of the head of some breeds.
Trace:	The dark line which runs down the spine of some short-coated breeds.
Tricolor:	A dog of three different colors, generally black, white and tan.
Trousers:	The hair on the hindquarters of some breeds, notably the Afghan.
Tucked-up:	When the loins are well lifted-up, as in the Greyhound.
Tulip ears:	Those ears which are carried erect, and lean slightly forwards.
Turn-up:	The projecting turned-up chin of the Bulldog.
Type:	That quality essential to a dog if he is to represent or approximate the ideal model of his breed based upon the Standard of the breed.
U.D.:	Utility dog. A dog trained for general services work.
Undercoat:	The soft, furry wool beneath the outer coat present in many breeds and sometimes of a different color.
Undershot:	Having the lower incisors projecting beyond the upper incisors, due to a malformation of the jaw, as in the Bulldog.
Unsound:	An unsound dog is one who is unhealthy or below average in general condition, working ability, movement or character. The unsoundness may be temporary or permanent, partial or complete. A bitch, after whelping, is temporarily unsound by being out of coat, etc. A deformed or unreliable dog is more or less permanently unsound.
Varminty:	A very bright or piercing expression.
Vent:	The tan colored hair situated under the tail of some breeds such as the Manchester Terrier. In a broader sense it is the area immediately surrounding the anus.

U.H.C.:	Very highly commended. An award granted to an exhibit of outstanding merit, but which generally carries no monetary prize with it. The award is fifth in order of placing.
Wall eyes:	Those which are parti-colored white-and-blue, normally seen in merle Sheepdogs and Collies and Cardigan Welsh Corgis.
Weedy:	Very lightly formed and lacking in substance.
Well sprung:	Well formed, with particular emphasis on chest development and spring or rib. When ribs are well rounded, sound and elastic, a dog is said to be well sprung.
Wheaten:	Color fawn or pale yellow.
Wheel back:	Another term for the arched or convex back.
Whelping:	The act of giving birth to puppies.
Whelps:	Newly born puppies.
Whip tail:	A tail which is stiff and straight, as in the Pointer when in action.
Whipcord tail:	One which is much too thin for the breed of dog to which it is attached. Distinct from the "string" tail of the Irish Water Spaniel.
Whole color:	One which covers the whole body as in red or black Cocker Spaniels.
Withers:	That point where the neck joins the body, about the shoulders.
Working certificate:	A certificate awarded to Gun-dogs at Field Trials where they have proved that they are trained and capable of carrying out the work for which they are bred. This award is necessary for any Gun-dog who is already a Show Champion and is required to be a Dual Champion.
Wrinkle:	Loosely folded skin on the forehead and cheeks.